W9-BKR-052

(continued)

Playing Their Way into Literacies
KAREN E. WOHLWEND

Teaching Literacy for Love and Wisdom
JEFFREY D. WILHELM & BRUCE NOVAK

Overtested
JESSICA ZACHER PANDYA

Restructuring Schools for Linguistic Diversity,
Second Edition
OFELIA B. MIRAMONTES, ADEL NADEAU, & NANCY L. COMMINS

Words Were All We Had
MARÍA DE LA LUZ REYES, ED.

Urban Literacies
VALERIE KINLOCH, ED.

Bedtime Stories and Book Reports
CATHERINE COMPTON-LILLY & STUART GREENE, EDS.

Envisioning Knowledge
JUDITH A. LANGER

Envisioning Literature, Second Edition
JUDITH A. LANGER

Writing Assessment and the Revolution in
Digital Texts and Technologies
MICHAEL R. NEAL

Artifactual Literacies
KATE PAHL & JENNIFER ROWSELL

Educating Emergent Bilinguals
OFELIA GARCÍA & JO ANNE KLEIFGEN

(Re)Imagining Content-Area Literacy Instruction
RONI JO DRAPER, ED.

Change Is Gonna Come
PATRICIA A. EDWARDS, GWENDOLYN THOMPSON MCMILLON, &
JENNIFER D. TURNER

When Commas Meet Kryptonite
MICHAEL BITZ

Literacy Tools in the Classroom
RICHARD BEACH, GERALD CAMPANO, BRIAN EDMISTON,
& MELISSA BORGMANN

Harlem on Our Minds
VALERIE KINLOCH

Teaching the New Writing
ANNE HERRINGTON, KEVIN HODGSON, & CHARLES MORAN, EDS.

Children, Language, and Literacy
CELIA GENISHI & ANNE HAAS DYSON

Children's Language
JUDITH WELLS LINDFORS

"You Gotta BE the Book," Second Edition
JEFFREY D. WILHELM

No Quick Fix
RICHARD L. ALLINGTON & SEAN A. WALMSLEY, EDS.

Children's Literature and Learning
BARBARA A. LEHMAN

Storytime
LARWRENCE R. SIPE

Effective Instruction for Struggling Readers, K–6
BARBARA M. TAYLOR & JAMES E. YSSELDYKE, EDS.

The Effective Literacy Coach
ADRIAN RODGERS & EMILY M. RODGERS

Writing in Rhythm
MAISHA T. FISHER

Reading the Media
RENEE HOBBS

teaching**media**literacy.com
RICHARD BEACH

What Was It Like?
LINDA J. RICE

Research on Composition
PETER SMAGORINSKY, ED.

The Vocabulary Book
MICHAEL F. GRAVES

Powerful Magic
NINA MIKKELSEN

New Literacies in Action
WILLIAM KIST

Teaching English Today
BARRIE R.C. BARRELL ET AL., EDS.

Bridging the Literacy Achievement Gap, 4–12
DOROTHY S. STRICKLAND & DONNA E. ALVERMANN, EDS.

Out of This World
HOLLY VIRGINIA BLACKFORD

Critical Passages
KRISTIN DOMBEK & SCOTT HERNDON

Making Race Visible
STUART GREENE & DAWN ABT-PERKINS, EDS.

The Child as Critic, Fourth Edition
GLENNA SLOAN

Room for Talk
REBEKAH FASSLER

Give Them Poetry!
GLENNA SLOAN

The Brothers and Sisters Learn to Write
ANNE HAAS DYSON

"Just Playing the Part"
CHRISTOPHER WORTHMAN

The Testing Trap
GEORGE HILLOCKS, JR.

Inquiry Into Meaning
EDWARD CHITTENDEN & TERRY SALINGER, WITH ANNE M. BUSSIS

"Why Don't They Learn English?"
LUCY TSE

Conversational Borderlands
BETSY RYMES

Inquiry-Based English Instruction
RICHARD BEACH & JAMIE MYERS

UNCOMMONLY
GOOD
IDEAS

Teaching Writing in the Common Core Era

SANDRA MURPHY

MARY ANN SMITH

Foreword by
Carol Jago

TEACHERS COLLEGE PRESS

TEACHERS COLLEGE | COLUMBIA UNIVERSITY
NEW YORK AND LONDON

NATIONAL WRITING PROJECT

National Writing Project
Berkeley, CA

Published simultaneously by Teachers College Press, 1234 Amsterdam Avenue, New York, NY 10027 and the National Writing Project, 2105 Bancroft Way, Berkeley, CA 94720-1042.

The National Writing Project (NWP) is a nationwide network of educators working together to improve the teaching of writing in the nation's schools and in other settings. NWP provides high-quality professional development programs to teachers in a variety of disciplines and at all levels, from early childhood through university. Through its network of nearly 200 university-based sites, NWP develops the leadership, programs, and research needed for teachers to help students become successful writers and learners.

Permission credit lines appear on page 154.

Library of Congress Cataloging-in-Publication Data

Murphy, Sandra (Sandra M.)
  Uncommonly good ideas-teaching : writing in the common core era / Sandra Murphy, Mary Ann Smith.
  pages cm
  Includes bibliographical references and index.
  ISBN 978-0-8077-5643-0 (pbk.)—ISBN 978-0-8077-7394-9 (ebook)
  1. English language—Composition and exercises—Study and teaching—United States. I. Title.
  LB1576.M863 2015
  808'.042071—dc23

                                                            2014046900

ISBN 978-0-8077-5643-0 (paper)
ISBN 978-0-8077-7394-9 (ebook)

Printed on acid-free paper
Manufactured in the United States of America

22 21 20 19 18 17 16 15   8 7 6 5 4 3 2 1

For the two Jims—
Jim Gray and Jim Moffett—
with gratitude for their wisdom
and unparalleled dedication to
teachers and to the teaching profession

Contents

Foreword

Most of us are intimidated by the idea of teaching writing. Though we are comfortable creating lessons around subject/verb agreement and parallel structure, what exactly does it mean to teach students how to write well? What does it look like? Sandra Murphy and Mary Ann Smith offer some uncommonly good ideas.

At the heart of this book is a belief in the power of writing. The authors view writing as both a vehicle for personal expression and a tool for effecting change. They also celebrate the pleasure that can come from producing a well-crafted piece. I was particularly struck by the attention they draw to the importance of pleasure within the learning process. Again and again I have observed that when my students were enjoying the writing task, they put in much more effort and as a result produced far better results.

Those students who love to write don't do so to improve their spelling or to practice using transitions. They write because it feels good. And because they often are keen to share what they've written, it suddenly becomes important to communicate clearly and to express one's ideas cogently. Communication gives purpose to correctness.

The ideas for teaching writing that Murphy and Smith offer are inspirational, not formulaic. They make it clear that "there is no magic, perfect, all-encompassing, sure-fire way to assemble a lesson . . . think of the upcoming lesson as representing one approach to integration. It's an adaptable model. Along the way we have suggested possible modifications and most certainly there is room for many more." *Uncommonly Good Ideas: Teaching Writing in the Common Core Era* provides readers with snapshots of excellent practice garnered from expert teachers in a variety of contexts. The application of these ideas is left to us.

In this Common Core era, many good ideas have been distorted and suddenly become new orthodoxies. Close reading is one example of an important practice that—unless we are careful—could devolve into a new set of instructional strategies that will do little to improve students' ability to read deeply. Another Common Core catch-phrase that is repeated so often that it has almost lost all meaning is *college and career readiness*. What does it mean to be ready? Shouldn't readiness include more than simply being able to make a living? What about readiness for the slings and arrows of outrageous fortune?

Murphy and Smith see versatility as a key to readiness in writing. They advocate a breadth of performances that build students' writing muscles across genre and audiences: "Students who can cozy up to a journal, craft a memoir, explain a process, and argue for a cause have a huge advantage. Their versatility will carry them a long way down the path to success in higher education and careers as well as the path to personal discovery."

Developing versatility as a writer takes time and practice. In too many classrooms—and for a variety of very good reasons, including class size—students do not get enough practice writing. This book will show you how to make peer response more effective, and give you ideas for handling the paper load and shifting responsibility for revision decisions from the teacher's shoulders to the writer's. As long as students depend on us to tell them what to change in a draft, their writing will never improve. We need to teach them how to read their own work with a critical eye and to ask themselves the questions a reader—or teacher—might ask.

As Murphy and Smith explain, "So many things to teach, so little time. So many books to read, so many papers to write, so many questions to answer, so many lives to touch. There isn't a teacher alive who doesn't struggle with how to slice up time, which always seems to be on backorder. The activities and assignments that develop students' versatility—activities such as reading, talking, listening, investigating, inquiring, analyzing, and practicing—are sure to gobble up more time than ever. There are few shortcuts when it comes to intellectual work." Amen to that. You will love the way this book gives you permission to take time to do the intellectual work you went into this profession for. I know I did.

Carol Jago

Acknowledgments

We especially wish to acknowledge the teachers who spent hours talking to us about their classroom practices:

Deborah Appleman
Barbara Buckley
Rebekah Caplan
John Davis
Tom Fox
Tracey Freyre
Jerome Halpern
Liz Harrington
Judy Kennedy
Zack Lewis-Murphy
Corine Maday
Jayne Marlink
Brendan Nelson
Gail Offen-Brown
Stephanie Paterson
Stan Pesick
Edna Shoemaker
Laura Stokes
Susan Threatt
Marleigh Williams

We also wish to thank the many other teachers whose names appear in this book and whose practices, stories, and insights contributed greatly to our professional conversation.

—Sandra Murphy and Mary Ann Smith, July 31, 2014

CHAPTER 1

Exploring Uncommonly Good Ideas in Teaching Writing

One trip through the travel section of your favorite bookstore and you might think everyone in the country is on a plane or in a car going somewhere. Printed guidebooks still own a lot of shelf space, even as many travelers now prefer to get their marching orders online. What's most surprising is that some tourists still haul around impossibly heavy guidebooks—thick as an old phonebook—that try to cover every possibility for what to see and do. And even if travelers don't intend to inspect every little sight and scene, they can get trapped into doing so.

We know a couple who recently traveled to South America. Their first stop was to be the Amazon in Peru. However, they arrived two days late because—you guessed it—their plane was delayed. So after hours in airports and on tarmacs, they had a singular view of what they wanted to do: shower and sleep.

The tour guides had a different idea. Not wanting their clients to miss one piece of flora and fauna, they figured out a way to turn a 4-day itinerary into a 2-day marathon. There was no time to unpack or even to move the suitcases beyond the hotel lobby. Instead, the guides herded everyone into vans, shuttling them from tree to tree for the next 14 hours. As the couple told us, "You get to the point of thinking, if you've seen one bird or monkey, you've seen them all. We could have settled for a postcard."

Whether it's a guidebook you can bench press or an overzealous tour guide, the result can be the same. Those travel pictures on your camera? When you get home and look at them, you can't remember exactly where you were.

An alternative for any exploration—whether of places or ideas—is to distinguish between the *must-see* attractions and the *maybes*. And in fact, in the world of teaching where even 14-hour days would be insufficient for covering everything in the guidebooks, the best alternative is to focus on the must-see.

TEACHING WRITING IS A MUST-SEE

Writing has a tendency to fall by the wayside when the curriculum gets too packed or when it narrows precipitously. Gallagher (2011) recalls that writing was one of the sacrificial lambs during past reform eras. In his words, writing was not only a "back burner" part of the curriculum, "in some cases writing [was] actually being removed from the stove completely" (p. 4).

Applebee et al. (2013) concur that writing can get lost in the shuffle:

> Buried in an avalanche of standards, curricular pacing guides, huge class sizes, worksheets, over-the-top testing, and, yes, even more testing (one teacher in Texas told me she now spends fifty-five days a year testing her students) writing—a necessity, a prerequisite to living a literate life—is not being given the time and attention it deserves. (p. 5)

Any teacher who experienced testing during the No Child Left Behind (NCLB) era knows all too well the ways it narrowed curriculum to the exclusion of writing. In fact, one could argue that test-taking skills became the heart of the curriculum. As Diane Ravitch (2011) recalls, "Test-taking skills took precedence over knowledge" (p. 107).

Writing may take a leave of absence from schools, but it certainly works overtime in our daily lives. It's the currency of so many of our personal and business communications—emails, text messages, Instagrams, Facebook, LinkedIn, and so on. (As we wrote this book, we became best friends with our local librarian through IChat.) On one hand, it's ironic that writing would ever take a back seat in the curriculum when it's so embedded in our culture. But inattention to writing is also outrageous. Who would ever think of getting students ready for college and for the world of work without teaching them to write? It would be like sending performers out on the stage before they had a chance to learn their lines.

"The reward of disciplined writing is the most valuable job attribute of all: a mind equipped to think. Writing today is not a frill for the few, but an essential skill for the many" (National Commission on Writing 2003, p. 11).

Writing is the big kahuna when it comes to being literate. Graham & Harris (2013) list the many reasons why writing is indispensable, such as its prominent role in sharing information; influencing and persuading others; helping us learn, understand, and remember; improving reading skills; expressing feelings; and even curing loneliness.

In fact, writing is more commonplace than ever. There was a day when the rite of passage in high school was the term paper. That was the moment when students *finally* took on serious subjects and began learning how to write with authority. That day has gone. People write volumes on the subway with their cellphones. They feel free to be experts on any subject and to blog and yelp and jabber online to anyone who will read their ideas and opinions. Writing is omnipresent:

. . . there is not a movie, advertising jingle, magazine, political campaign, news-paper, theatrical production, hit record, comic book, or instructional manual that does not begin with writers and rest on writing. Popular culture and the economies of the Western world depend on writing today in ways hard to imagine even a few generations ago. Although only a few hundred thousand adults earn their living as full-time writers, many working Americans would not be able to hold their positions if they were not excellent writers. . . . More than 90 percent of midcareer professionals recently cited the "need to write effectively" as a skill "of great importance" in their day-to-day work. (National Commission on Writing, 2003, pp. 10–11)

WRITING IN THE ERA OF THE COMMON CORE

During a recent Writing Project institute at the University of California–Berkeley (UC Berkeley), teacher–participants celebrated the idea that writing is back in fashion, due in part to the Common Core State Standards (CCSS). Their enthusiasm fell short of a pep rally, however, because everyone felt a little rusty. It has been a while since teachers have been able to pull out all the stops when it comes to writing. One teacher, who undoubtedly spoke for so many others, coined her own refrain: "But where do I start?"

If they aren't inundated now, teachers will soon be buffeted by a barrage of "Common Core aligned" materials—in print, online, and at conference sessions. There will be new lists of do's and don'ts and new caveats about what is acceptable and unacceptable. When the flood gates open, teachers will need some means of sorting out what really matters and of getting in touch with the must-see strategies and approaches to teaching writing.

Certainly the writers of the CCSS came to their task thinking about must-see ideas. One of the problems they attempted to address was the tendency for standards to turn into bite-sized pieces, little chunks of knowledge and skills that teachers and students must digest in a certain order. They recognized that past approaches fragmented the curriculum so that no item of importance got its due. Kelly Gallagher remembers the fallout:

In an attempt to teach an unrealistic number of standards, a vast majority of schools in this country are driving students through an unrealistic amount of material, putting a lot of pressure on educators to spend an unrealistic time preparing for multiple-choice exams, resulting in scores printed in the newspaper that give parents an unrealistic notion of how prepared (or, more accurately, unprepared) their children are upon exiting school. (2011, p. 4)

To avoid these kinds of potholes, the CCSS writers aimed for "fewer, higher, deeper" with the anchor standards, 10 broad umbrella statements about goals for student learning. They refrained from telling teachers how to put these goals into operation in the classroom—a complete 180 degrees from the era of scripts and pacing guides:

> The Standards define what all students are expected to know and be able to do, not how teachers should teach. (Council of Chief State School Officers [CCSSO] & the National Governors Association [NGA], 2010, p. 9)

But we know what happens with standards when the vision and the reality collide. They go though some mysterious multiplication and division process and end up on someone's whiteboard with check marks. Like the weary travelers in the Amazon, teachers get herded into vans that rush from place to place and linger nowhere. Then there are the assessments that divvy up performances and complex thinking into discrete, decontextualized test items to fit a multiple-choice format. That's when the collective education system overreacts and everything—from the curriculum to the bulletin boards—begins to resemble the test.

Whether or not these standards will come to resemble their predecessors, we think they contain some real gold for teaching and learning to write. In the flurry that accompanies any new reform effort, the must-sees can get lost. In this book we concentrate on those must-sees—several big ideas that are, not by accident, major themes that appear in the CCSS English language arts (ELA) standards and in countless other research and best practice publications, not to mention in writing classrooms.

Here are some of the center-stage approaches to teaching writing:

- Integrating reading, writing, speaking, and listening
- Teaching writing as a process
- Extending the range of students' writing and writing experiences
- Spiraling
- Scaffolding
- Collaborating

These uncommonly good ideas are not new to every teacher. But they carry a different weight with the CCSS in play. They're officially back in town.

What's more, this list may look suspiciously familiar: like "old" practices now rising from the ashes or maybe from the recycling bin. It's true. These are enduring practices—ones that have stood the test of time because, in addition to supporting young student authors in the classroom, these practices inhabit the writing lives of professional authors. It's no surprise, for instance, that published writers throw themselves into a full-time reading-writing-speaking-listening routine. People who write for a living integrate the language arts as a matter of course.

Journalists, for example, work from multiple interviews and conversations with experts, eye-witnesses, and men and women on the street. Their job is to sift through as much evidence as possible—reading, researching, asking questions, and fact checking—before they submit their stories. Robert Caro, for one, who trained to be a journalist before he became a biographer, employs the finest of literary integration techniques.

> In his New York City office, where everything has its particular place, he works long hours, seven days a week, poring through interview transcripts and primary source notes, working slowly and deliberately on books he publishes, on average, once every 10 years. His meticulous routine is sometimes painful, he says, but necessary. (Darman, 2009)

Professional writers also have highly developed, often idiosyncratic ways of scaffolding their writing—little props, elaborate rituals, superstitions, and techniques they've developed that help them get words on the page.

They might write standing, instead of sitting (Ernest Hemingway, Thomas Wolfe, Virginia Woolf, and Lewis Carroll). Benjamin Franklin wrote while soaking in a bathtub. Balzac drank excessive amounts of coffee, more than 50 cups a day, and according to Ackerman, "actually died from caffeine poisoning"(Ackerman, 1989, p. 1). Modern-day author Stephen King depends on a particular setup: a glass of water, a vitamin pill, music, and papers that are arranged in a certain place (Rogak, 2009). The goal of all these techniques, offbeat as they may sound, is to focus the mind and get in the zone for writing.

Professional writers are often risk takers and experimenters, stretching themselves by trying out new kinds of writing or new ways to write. Herman Wouk, the author of *The Caine Mutiny*, *Marjorie Morningstar*, *Youngblood Hawke*, and *The Winds of War*, had uncanny personal success as a writer. Many of his headliners became movies, and he won the Pulitzer Prize for *The Caine Mutiny*. At age 97, he wrote yet another novel, *The Lawgiver*, a complete departure from his others because he developed the characters and told the story through letters, memos, emails, journals, news articles, recorded talk, Skype transcripts, and text messages. Clearly, Wouk was several generations removed from the social networkers, and in fact, he did not communicate through text messages. But that fact did not stop him from expanding the range of his writing.

The obvious message is this: Writers (with a capital W) are probably the inventors of the big ideas. And if they didn't invent processes like drafting and revising, practices like speaking, reading, and writing in tandem, and settings/setups that help the words flow, they certainly hang onto them through thick and thin. So, yes, the teaching practices that show up in this book are tried and true; they have been around for decades, maybe even centuries. They may come and go occasionally when school reformers take education in a different direction, but they never disappear altogether.

The trick is to keep them front and center. The CCSS document for English Language Arts and Literacy in History/Social Studies, Science, and Technical Subjects contains 66 pages, and the appendices are more than four times that long. That's a lot to digest and none of it is exactly bedtime reading. And truth be told, if the "fewer, higher, deeper" ideas in the CCSS get deconstructed and reconstructed into fragments or isolated skills or anything that resembles multiple guess, then we are right back in the crazed-tour-guide approach to standards. Our task in this book, then, is to mine the gold in the writing standards so teachers can go for the teaching approaches that will have the biggest payoff.

One other advantage to focusing on the big ideas: We can skirt around and possibly even debunk some of the inevitable mythology about the CCSS. In "The Common Core Ate My Baby and Other Urban Legends," Timothy Shanahan (2013) explores the idea that the CCSS have "given rise to anxieties among educators that have fueled the flames of misperception, confusion, and rumor" (p. 10). Even as he tries to dismantle some of the myths, Shanahan demonstrates how difficult rumors are to squash. For example, one of the misunderstandings has to do with difficult reading material. Some folks think there's now a blanket rule that all texts need to be difficult to the point of utter frustration for students. Shanahan attempts to counter this view:

> Even with older students, the idea is not to have students reading challenging texts exclusively. Students should have an array of reading experiences in the same way that a long-distance runner has a varied training schedule that intersperses different distances and speeds. These varied schedules enable the runner to build muscle, speed, and endurance. (p. 14)

We go along with Shanahan. And whether or not we can successfully reassure teachers that they will not have to throw out both baby and bathwater, we do promise to poke a little fun at the standards and to take a common sense approach to addressing them. We know all too well what Elliot Eisner (1985) speaks of when he says, "one is struck by the sober, humorless quality of so much of the writing in the field of curriculum and in educational research" (p. 20). We try, then, to spare our readers the magisterial approach to the CCSS.

One more note. It may seem that the big ideas stand alone. We talk about them separately, but in operation they work hand in hand. Collaboration is part of writing as a process; integration involves scaffolding; extending the range of student writing requires spiraling; and so on.

ENTERING INTO A PROFESSIONAL CONVERSATION

Teachers read about themselves everywhere—what they should be doing that they're not doing, what they shouldn't be doing that they are doing. When it comes to education, everyone weighs in. The real mischief is that many of those comments oversimplify an extremely complicated enterprise, one that Lee Shulman (2004) compares to moments of crisis in medicine:

> The only time a physician could possibly encounter a situation of comparable complexity would be in the emergency room of a hospital during or after a natural disaster. (p. 258)

> After some 30 years of doing such work, I have concluded that classroom teaching—particularly at the elementary and secondary levels—is perhaps the most complex, most challenging, and most demanding, subtle, nuanced, and frightening activity that our species has ever invented. (p. 504)

What's more, teachers have just emerged from a didactic reform era during which they were treated as conduits for a hand-me-down curriculum. The time for professional conversation is long overdue.

We started our work on this book by having our own professional conversations with dozens of teachers. We asked them about their practices—especially the ones that incorporate some of the big ideas—not because of the CCSS, but because these ideas worked in their classrooms. Many, but not all, had participated in the Writing Project. All are teachers who think deeply about their practice and who are knowledgeable and engaged as professionals. From our point of view, teachers are essential participants in any conversation about teaching.

We've included some college teachers in the mix, those who teach 1st-year writing classes to 18-year-olds. In doing so, we had the Writing Project philosophy in mind: teachers teaching teachers across grade levels, giving each other a broader picture of how teaching and learning to write evolve. For secondary teachers, especially those who teach the same 18-year-olds—separated only by a summer—we want to provide a look at how their college counterparts work through familiar challenges in the teaching of writing. We believe these examples are particularly appropriate in the CCSS climate for the following reasons:

- They create a transparent link between high school and college.
- They are relevant and useful in helping students become "college ready."
- They are adaptable for different populations of students.

- Many high school teachers already use online college materials as well as materials supplied by the College Board for Advanced Placement courses and by local colleges and universities.

We've also tried to represent the diversity of classrooms in which teachers work by including English language arts teachers from urban, rural, and suburban schools; teachers of English language learners (ELLs); history teachers; and health and career/technical education teachers. Collectively, the teachers work with students whose abilities and experiences vary widely.

Our stories about teachers take the form of case studies. These are not formal studies by any means. Their purpose is to illustrate how uncommonly good ideas look in the classroom and how teachers think about what goes on there. We refer often to the notion of an intellectual or professional community—a space where teachers can share, learn, write, and solve problems together. To the extent that any book can be a catalyst for such a community, we hope this one might make some small contribution.

We start off in Chapter 2 with a full-blown lesson, designed around teaching narrative writing. It illustrates some tried and true, sequenced practices for teaching writing as a process, ones that teachers have used for decades in their classrooms. While we continue to comment on lesson design, we do not present a step-by-step lesson beyond Chapter 2. Rather the remaining chapters explore a broad range of teaching approaches that help students tackle different kinds of writing and understand complexities like audience and purpose.

Finally, we chose to write about food. Yes, you read that right. In the next two chapters of this book we use food as the topic for the lessons. People of all ages and cultures have surprisingly intense memories about food and its importance in their lives with families and friends. It's a subject that spans many disciplines, for example, history, science, psychology, health, anthropology, even math. We think that sticking to the same topic— in this case food—makes it easier for readers to see a progression from one kind of writing to another or from one writing challenge to another. The topic of food lends itself to both fiction and nonfiction reading and writing. On the other hand, any topic can be distracting to a reader who is trying to picture teaching a particular group of students or a particular curriculum, so we offer a broader range of topics for writing in Chapters 4 and 5.

LAST THOUGHTS

It goes without saying that teachers are not just teaching writing. They are teaching students with all their marvelous diversity and with all the languages and life experiences they bring to the classroom. Students cannot be standardized and turned out for distribution like cans of tomatoes. Even

> "If you find you are having trouble writing and nothing seems real, just write about food. It is always solid and is the one thing we all can remember about our day." (Goldberg, 2010, pp. 138-139)

the best ideas in the world for teaching writing and learning to write may not always work for every student, especially since students grow in fits and starts and not necessarily at the same rate. One of our favorite teacher authors, Jane Juska (1989), had this to say about her struggling 9th-graders:

> My students do not write in pages. They write in inches, or half-inches. Sometimes, with great efforts on their parts and mine, they write as much as a half a foot. (p. 13)

Juska also notes that students are fully aware when their writing doesn't measure up and they find creative ways to make it disappear.

> Sometimes it [writing] becomes origami, beautiful birds that sail across the room. Or it may turn into a sleek airplane, its nose cutting into the space somewhere above my head. Or it turns into a basketball, crumpled round, arcing into the wastepaper basket. (p. 13)

It might sound like teaching writing is an endless uphill battle, and, for sure, there isn't a standards document, either on the shelf or currently in play, that mentions a word about enjoyment—either for students or teachers.

This reminds us that years ago an evaluator of the National Writing Project (NWP) gave a satisfaction survey to institute participants each summer to gauge the effectiveness and relevance of their experience. Over time, this evaluation tool took on an unofficial name: the happiness survey. Eventually, funders of the Writing Project asked for something different, something along the quasi-experimental line. Once the survey disappeared, teachers joked that happiness was out the door. Who needs to be happy?

We are here to say that happiness and having fun in the classroom matters a lot. As Donald Murray (1985) says, "It is time to give away the secret: teaching writing is fun" (p. 1).

CHAPTER 2

Integrating the Language Arts

Using reading, writing, speaking, and listening in concert with each other is the natural order of things. It's the way we work in the world, the way we do business. Even something as everyday as planning a party can throw the planners into a swirl of language activities. We know a recently married couple who wanted a special celebration for friends and family several months after their courthouse ceremony. We'll call them Kumar and Sara.

Because the groom is originally from India, where his family still lives, the couple wanted to serve Indian food. They checked out caterers and menus, as any one of us might, by consulting the Internet. But even the groom couldn't vouch for the spiciness of things that popped up on nearly every source, like the *allo goby* (cauliflower, potatoes, ginger, garlic, herbs, and spices).

The bride began to get cold feet. As part of the search, she landed on several articles about Indian food. Words like *hot*, *salty*, and *pungent* jumped out at her, along with the phrase "recipe for indigestion." And that's when the talking and writing began. Sara and Kumar went from restaurant to restaurant, sampling food and asking questions. Sara took notes and Kumar kept his eye on her spelling of Indian foods. They emailed various caterers and also family members, asking for advice. They sent each other long messages during the day while they were at work, trying out ideas and sharing new sources. In one email Sarah suggested to Kumar that they limit the Indian portion of their menu to the hors d'oeuvres. The deciding communication was a text message: *R U up 4 American food?*

Notice that no one assigned Sara and Kumar to read before they wrote, or to rope off their talk from their research, or to make a separate list of their spelling and vocabulary words. Instead, the modes of reading, writing, speaking, and listening spurred each other on, and made it possible for Sara and Kumar to plan their party.

In school, the practice of integrating the language arts may not be so easy.

If one were asked to name three things that are the hardest for schools to bring about, the answer would most likely be individualization, interaction, and integration. This is because the trend of any institution, not just of schools, goes the other way—toward standardization, isolation, and compartmentalization. (Moffett & Wagner, 1976, p. 42)

Moffett and Wagner go on to say that children learn and use language "through everything, all the time, and with everybody. Learning is not thought of as a specialized activity and is not restricted to a certain time, place, people and circumstance" (p. 43).

Certainly, the party-planning story supports Moffett and Wagner's point. All the hubbub about menus happened at once, the way spices mingle in an Indian dish. No wonder duplicating such a scene in the classroom might seem difficult and unmanageable.

In this chapter we put the idea of integration to work in a lesson design for narrative writing—one that incorporates writing process techniques as well. Sticking with one design makes it easier to see how teaching and learning build in a logical sequence and how reading, writing, speaking, and listening flow naturally together. On the other hand, there is no magic, perfect, all-encompassing, sure-fire way to assemble a lesson. So, as a final caveat before we dig in, think of the upcoming lesson as representing one approach to integration. It's an adaptable model. Along the way we have suggested possible modifications and most certainly there is room for many more.

ADVANTAGES OF INTEGRATING THE LANGUAGE ARTS

Probably most of us have experienced personally the challenge of writing a cover letter to accompany our resume. Typically, this task causes a writer to fret because the audience is unknown, the sell-yourself contents are supposed to amplify but not duplicate the resume, the situation is competitive, and whether or not time is a factor, the outcome is at stake. Who among us would tackle this chore cold without a model or a friend's advice or some kind of guidance?

Seldom does the writing muse do a solo dance. It takes a flurry of language activity—the quartet of reading, writing, speaking, and listening—to move our ideas forward. In particular, the bond between reading and writing has been well documented. James Gray, the founder of the National Writing Project, was fond of describing reading and writing as "two sides of the same coin." Simply stated, reading helps writing and writing helps reading. For example, Colvin-Murphy (1986) found that students who wrote when they read "remembered more, were more engaged in thinking about what they were reading, and were more sensitive to the author's craft" (quoted in Tierney, Caplan, Ehri, Healy, and Hurdlow, 1989, pp. 191–192).

It seems almost indisputable that reading and writing fuel and fortify each other, in part because they depend on the same cognitive processes (Fitzgerald & Shanahan, 2000; Shanahan, 2006; Tierney & Shanahan, 1996). Summarizing more than 30 years of various studies, Duke, Pearson, Strachan, and Billman (2011) say that "Research confirms that exemplary teachers who produce high-achieving readers and writers tend to integrate the two domains regularly and thoroughly in the classroom" (p. 76).

However, in the pendulum of reform movements, teachers have sometimes had little choice but to teach reading in isolation. In these cases, writing has been turned into a wallflower, the neglected kid at the 7th-grade dance. In the recent era of packaged teaching materials and hyperemphasis on reading, writing languished in schools once again. (The irony is that many students have been writing up a storm outside of school with their emails, instant messages, and blogs.) Even if teachers had wanted to toss a teaspoon of writing into a reading-only program, they had little chance to do so. As teacher Brandy DeAlba points out, "For the last decade teachers have read from a script that actually says, 'smile here'" (personal communication, July 9, 2014). Colleague Karen Smith adds, "I know of districts where every teacher had to be on the same page on the same day" (personal communication, July 9, 2014).

Aside from the fact that a reading-only curriculum denies students the very tools they need to become accomplished readers—like writing and talking—it also has other unfortunate consequences. More than 20 years ago, James Moffett noted that "in favoring reading over writing, schools have not only made both harder to master, but have necessarily also made students more the consumers of others' thinking than original thinkers themselves" (Moffett, 1989b, p. 21).

In contrast to a segregated approach, the CCSS integrate the language arts. While the anchor standards are divided into reading, writing, speaking, and listening strands for clarity (and to keep the reader from throwing in the towel) the document clearly states "the processes of communication are closely connected . . ." (CCSSO & NGA, 2010, p. 4).

Of course, integrating the language arts should not depend on a set of standards. Nor should it be a luxury item, something to buy in good times and discard during recessions or changes in fashion, although it has come and gone from classrooms like polka dots from the runway. The challenge for contemporary teachers, as NCLB takes its last gasp, is to resuscitate the connections between reading, writing, speaking, and listening. But that's not all. Because language in all its forms is the centerpiece of communicating digitally, teachers have the additional task of teaching students how integration plays out in the world of technology. And since research is at the fingertips of anyone with a computer, tablet, or smart phone, teachers have yet a third charge: integrating the skill and habit of looking things up, whether at lightning speed or in a slower, more cumulative way.

CAPTURING THE BIG IDEA OF INTEGRATION

Years ago the late Donald M. Murray, a writer and a teacher of writing, challenged a group of Bay Area Writing Project teachers at UC Berkeley to rethink the first day of school. "Forget reviewing the tardy policy," he said. "Save all the class rules for later. Start things right off. Ask your students to write, and you write with them."

Murray suggested that after an adequate time for some real writing, teachers invite students to read their writing to the class. He admonished teachers to wait out the silence. "There's always some extroverted kid who will come forward." At some point the teacher will have to read his or her writing too, Murray insisted.

As if reading the big question "WHY?" in the minds of his audience, Murray laid out the reasons for taking a risk like this one. Writing on the very first day sets the tone for the rest of the year. It introduces the idea of a community of writers. And in one fell swoop, students and their teacher are reading, writing, speaking, and listening to each other.

And that's the point of this chapter. We will explore ways to mix it up, to design writing lessons that deliberately immerse students in the full spectrum of the language arts.

TAKING THE PLUNGE:
FIRST STEPS IN AN INTEGRATED LESSON DESIGN

The CCSS specify three broad categories of writing—narrative, informational, and argumentative—without suggesting a particular order for teaching them, or for that matter, a way to teach them. "Teachers are thus free to provide students with whatever tools and knowledge their professional judgment and experience identify as most helpful for meeting the goals set out in the Standards" (CCSSO & NGA, 2010, p. 4).

Easy to say. Brenda Cartagena, a New York teacher with 13 years of experience, explains that "many teachers, especially new ones, are feeling overwhelmed. . . . They [CCSS] just told us, this is the expectation, and you figure it out" (Merrow, 2013).

Figuring it out will take a village. Our village is the National Writing Project network, where teachers have collaborated for 40 years. Well before the Common Core State Standards came to town, these teachers designed integrated writing lessons. In this chapter we offer a lesson design based on what we have learned from them over the years and from research on best practices in the teaching of writing. Figure 2.1 on the next page illustrates the fundamental elements of this lesson design.

Figure 2.1. Basic Features of the Lesson Design

- Starters or warm-ups
- Craft workshops with mentor texts and try-it-on writing
- Reading in preparation for a final writing assignment
- Drafting a final writing assignment
- Revising with peer response groups
- Mini craft workshop during revision
- Celebration and publication!

Here are other things to know about the upcoming lesson design:

1. It's one model in a world of infinite models.
2. It integrates reading, writing, speaking, and listening.
3. It takes students through a writing process.
4. It suggests a general order of activities, not to be confused with a lockstep sequence.
5. It focuses on narrative writing.

Starting the year with narrative is a comfortable choice for so many of us. Who doesn't love a story? But there are other reasons to do so. Narrative is central to examining our own experiences and to analyzing the lessons they offer. "Real learning emerges from sorting, analyzing, and evaluating the stuff of everyday life. Through examining a personal experience critically and carefully, writers develop a fuller sense of their own identity and their own power as thinking, feeling human beings" (California Department of Education, 1993, p. 11).

Narrative often shows up in other kinds of writing. It adds human interest, supports claims, illustrates and explains ideas, and provides examples. Narrative brings informational and argumentative writing to life with phrases such as "in my experience," "I remember when . . . ," or "My grandmother always said . . ."

A final reminder about our lesson design: It can be tailored to fit different needs and teachers should not feel constrained by the particular topics we have chosen.

For Starters

Starters help students build content and enthusiasm for their writing. At their best, they draw on reading, writing, speaking, and listening.

It hasn't always been the case that reading and writing assignments include some kind of preactivity. Many of us remember the day when we opened a book like *A Tale of Two Cities* without any kind of introduction or preparation for the opening gambit: "It was the best of times, it was the worst of times, it was the age of wisdom, it was the age of foolishness." Fortunately, tapping into and augmenting students' prior knowledge is no longer a new idea.

In the same vein, prewriting—once considered "touchy-feely"—is now a recognized staple in the writing classroom. Researcher Steve Graham, for one, looked at multiple studies of what makes a difference to student writing. Prewriting showed up as a key element of effective writing instruction:

> Pre-writing engages students in activities designed to help them generate or organize ideas for their composition. Engaging adolescents in such activities before they write a first draft improves the quality of their writing. (Graham & Perin, 2007, p. 18)

As a way into a topic or concept, starters do more than whet the appetite. They give students the chance to warm up with ideas that are close to home. When students fill in a chart like the one in Figure 2.2, they are engaging in individual brainstorming, recalling and sorting their experiences for possible use. Starters are even more effective when students share, for example, selecting one item from their list to present to the rest of the class.

Figure 2.2. A Starter for Writing About Food

TYPE OF FOOD	YOUR CHOICE OF FOOD
Your favorite food	
A food you dislike	
Foods for special occasions	
A fast food you crave	
A comfort food	
A food recently new to you	
Healthy foods you like	
Cultural foods	
Foods you make yourself	
Food from a box or can	

Thoughts on Lesson Design

Whether the writing topic is about split pea soup or global warming, this kind of opener asks students to recall and roll out, bit by bit, what they

Figure 2.3. Ideas for Starters

talking	listing
researching	brainstorming
free or quick writing	reading what other students have written
visualizing	
drawing	deciding on purpose and audience
clustering or mapping	interviewing
outlining	looking at models
role-playing	watching a video
asking questions	revisiting portfolio entries
writing in a journal	

know at this moment about that topic. By sharing one item on their lists, students open up possibilities for their classmates to "borrow" ideas. The pool of knowledge grows and is available to everyone. When all the ideas are on the table, students can try their hand at one that interests them. Right away students are mixing it up, with each other, and with all the language arts processes in play. They are getting a whiff of content and generating more as they go.

Generally speaking, starters are fast. As Figure 2.3 indicates, they are not the main event. Further, not every warm-up strategy works with every writer or task. Some students actually take to outlining, while others would find outlining a guaranteed brain freezer. In the end, we want students to internalize and use the strategies that work best for them (when the teacher is not even in the room).

DIVING DEEPER:
CRAFT WORKSHOP WITH MENTOR TEXTS AND TRY-IT-ON WRITING

Short, embedded lessons or workshops on craft can introduce, revisit, or expand techniques/skills for writing.

Mentor texts are ideal for demonstrating new strategies and formats. At their best they serve as models of good writing and offer a concrete way into teaching craft—the tools and techniques for constructing a particular piece of writing. In short, mentor texts serve as a blueprint for students to try on new techniques.

As a lead-in for the following mentor text assignment, students might return to their list of personal food preferences and do a 5-minute quick-write on a food they dislike. They can describe the food and explain their aversion to it. As a second lead-in, the teacher might do some kind of fast class poll of Jell-O lovers versus Jell-O skeptics. What makes the lovers love Jell-O? Why are the skeptics skeptical?

Mentor Text: "Lost in Translation"

Author Monique Truong (2010) writes about her first encounter with Jell-O salad at the home of an American family living in North Carolina. Even though Truong and her family experienced unnamed terrors as they escaped from Vietnam, they were nevertheless stumped and appalled by a seemingly harmless American food:

> We were horrified, which was really saying something considering that this man, woman, and child had only months before escaped from a country at war. Jell-O, jarred mayo, grated carrots, and a handful of raisins molded into a glistening, wobbly, neon-bright ring can do that: scare the pants off an unsuspecting Vietnamese refugee family. . . .
>
> It flickers in my imagination like a Super-8 film: the Jell-O salad, aglow with artificial food coloring, beckoning from the center of the table. A silver-plated pie server cuts a slab, which hovers and then jiggles onto my plate. I know my mother is keeping a watchful eye on me, making sure that I, like her, take a polite bite or two. I avoid the bottom layer, opaque with mayonnaise and whipped gelatin, and go for the iridescent dome, flecked and studded with vegetables and fruits. (p. 1)

After the reading, students can highlight or underline the specific details that "show" what the food looked like. What are the details that make the food scary? This will be an easy task for most students, who have likely experienced the idea of "show, don't tell" in elementary school. They will identify the adjectives—for example, glistening, wobbly, neon-bright—and active verbs—hovers, jiggles. The most astute may notice that the writer gives the Jell-O human powers: It can beckon. And finally, students may recognize that the writer dramatizes her polite bite by using specific details (mayonnaise, gelatin, iridescent dome) and by a snippet of action (server cuts a slab . . . my mother is keeping a watchful eye . . . I, like her, take a polite bite).

Thoughts on Lesson Design

Why return to "show, don't tell" with secondary students? The purpose is generally the same with both younger and older students—to teach them strategies they can use in all of their writing, whether narrative, informational, or argumentative. However, for secondary students, returning to an old lesson comes with new challenges: how to ramp up knowledge and control. This means students should be able to do the following things:

Anton Chekov illustrates the idea of "show, don't tell." "Don't tell me the moon is shining; show me the glint of light on broken glass." (quoted in Donovan, 2015)

- Retrieve strategies when they need them
- Identify strategies in their own and in other people's writing
- Use strategies intentionally in drafting and revising
- Pinpoint and develop a character, an emotion, or a moment in time

Try-It-On Writing

> Short practice assignments invite students to try out what they are learning
> and to share their draft with a peer for targeted feedback.

The following writing task gives students a chance to manipulate "show, don't tell" strategies. At this point, students have identified several that work well in narrative: well-chosen adjectives, active verbs, specific identifiable details, and bits of action. They also might want to experiment with giving their subject human powers. Keeping a running list of such strategies—whether individually or as a class—is useful.

"Show Don't Tell" Prompt

Think of a food that puzzled or horrified you. Show your reader how it looked and tasted. You can include the ingredients, as author Monique Truong does in her description of Jell-O. Be sure to let your reader know why you found this particular food to be so strange or frightening.

You will be trading your paper with another student and from your "show, don't tell" writing, your reader will judge whether the food or the food experience falls into the category of truly horrifying and/or puzzling.

Thoughts on Lesson Design

The value of this "try-it-on" writing experience lies in the doing and the sharing afterward. Teacher Rebekah Caplan (1984) developed a daily writing program for middle and high school students that emphasized "show, don't tell" exercises, followed by public performance—reading aloud some of the student papers, identifying effective techniques, and making suggestions of other possible techniques. Caplan notes that students "assimilate new ideas for specificity by regularly hearing other students' writing" (p. 14).

The purpose of this workshop is for students to solidify and remember the strategies they used in their try-on. Sharing their papers or hearing them read aloud brings the strategies home one more time. Best of all, students are once again immersed in language interaction.

A word of caution. When students try out strategies that are new to them, they can sometimes overdo a good thing. Caplan notes that " students often do get carried away with description." However, Caplan says, "I would much rather have them overdescribe than underdevelop. With regular response and evaluation from teachers and peers, students prone to overdoing it can learn to cut back and edit" (p. 26).

This kind of craft workshop with try-it-on writing has advantages for teachers as well. Caplan does not bend over a stack of papers each night, forcing herself to come up with grades and comments. Rather, she gives students credit for their efforts and selectively grades a certain number of papers on the spot each day, in particular the ones she chooses to read out loud. In other words, this is a teaching and learning event, not a back-breaker for either the teacher or the student.

DIVING IN AGAIN:
MORE PRACTICE WITH "SHOWING" TECHNIQUES

The workshop that follows gives students a second crack at writing with specifics. The rationale for doing a second practice round, if time permits, is that students often need the repetition and, in this case, the chance to expand the strategies available to them for showing, not telling.

Both of the following narratives deal with the subject of school lunch and offer models of "showing" techniques. Both have the same theme: There are social expectations around school lunches that prescribe right and wrong ways of doing things.

> Mae West said, "Too much of a good thing can be wonderful." The good thing here is practice and more practice to build skill and confidence.

As a lead-in for the reading excerpts, students can pair up and share what they remember from their childhoods about school lunches. What was a really good thing about school lunches (sitting next to a friend, sharing food, going home for lunch, finding a special treat) and what were some not-so-good things (noise, standing in line, cafeteria food, feeling rushed)?

Mentor Text: *Bird By Bird: Some Instructions On Writing And Life*

Anne Lamott (1995) writes about the "rules" of school lunches—what kids once considered "cool" and "not cool."

Your sandwich was the centerpiece, and there were strict guidelines. It almost goes without saying that store-bought white bread was the only acceptable bread. There were no exceptions. If your mother made the white bread for your sandwich, you could only hope that no one would notice. You certainly did not brag about it, any more than you would brag that she also made headcheese. And there were only a few things that your parents could put in between the two pieces of bread. Bologna was fine, salami and unaggressive cheese were fine, peanut butter and jelly were fine if your parents understood the jelly/jam issue.

Grape jelly was best, by far, a nice slippery comforting sugary petroleum-product grape. Strawberry jam was second; everything else was iffy. (p. 35)

In general, come to think of it, when fathers made lunches, things always turned out badly. Fathers were so oblivious back then. They were like foreigners. For instance, a code bologna sandwich meant white bread, one or two slices of bologna, mustard, one wilted piece of iceberg lettuce. (The Catholics were heavily into mayonnaise, which we might get into later.) Fathers, to begin with, always used nonregulation bread and then buttered it, which made the sandwich about as tradable as a plate of haggis. Also, everything was always falling out of the sandwiches fathers made. I'm not sure why. They'd use anything green and frilly for lettuce, when of course only the one piece of wilted iceberg was permissible. Your friends saw a big leaf of romaine falling out along with the slice of bologna, and you might soon find yourself alongside the kid against the fence. (p. 36)

Thoughts on Lesson Design

In this excerpt about school lunches, Lamott uses three techniques that students can identify and add to their list of key ways that authors connect with readers through showing, not telling. The first technique is to define something by naming what it is and what it is not. Working individually or in pairs, students can jot down or otherwise highlight the details that define a code lunch (store-bought white bread, bologna, salami, unaggressive cheese, peanut butter with either grape jelly or strawberry jam), along with details about what violates the code lunch rules (homemade white bread, buttered bread, romaine lettuce, or anything other than iceberg).

Lamott's second technique is to characterize a group of people, in this case fathers, for humorous effect. Not to be forgotten is Lamott's use of comparison, technique number three in this excerpt. Fathers, bless them, are like foreigners, or at least they were "back in the day."

> Paired readings on the same subject offer still more "showing" techniques.

Mentor Text: *Stealing Buddha's Dinner*

Bich Minh Nguyen (2007) writes about school lunches from the point of view of a young Vietnamese immigrant. Again, school lunches are accompanied by strict standards.

At [elementary school], whatever academic success I had was completely eroded at lunchtime. Here, a student was measured by the contents of her lunch bag, which displayed status, class, and parental love. I didn't tell any-one that I packed my own lunch, but the girls in my grade figured it out. "My mom loves to pack my lunch," said Sara Jonkman, whose hard blue eyes emitted a vicious spark.

The anxiety of what to pack weighed on me every school week. The key was to have at least one shining element: a plain sandwich and baggie of po-tato chips could be made tolerable with the right dessert snack. If the planets and grocery sales aligned in my favor, I might even have a Hostess Cupcake. All morning I would look forward to peeling away the flat layer of deep chocolate frosting decorated with one lovely white squiggle. This I set aside while I ate the cake, licking out the cream filling, sighing over the richness, the darkness of the crumbs. Then at last I could focus on the frosting, taking small bites around the white squiggle, which must always be saved as long as possible. I imagined careful bakers hovering over each cupcake, forming the curlicue design with unerring precision. Beneath the status of Hostess Cupcakes were Ho Hos, Ding Dongs, Devil Squares, Zingers, and Little Debbie Fudge Brownies. The lower tier, just above generic cookies, included the cloying Oatmeal Crème Pies, SnoBalls, Star Crunches, and Twinkies. (pp. 75–76)

Thoughts on Lesson Design

One of the simplest techniques for showing, but one that is often over-looked by student writers, is the use of proper nouns. What does a proper noun do for a reader that a common noun cannot? It creates in the read-er's mind a specific image. For example, Nguyen's phrase "dessert snack" does not evoke much of a mental picture as does the proper noun Hostess Cupcake or Twinkie. But Nguyen also gives her list of proper nouns a special touch. She fashions a hierarchy of snacks, each of them named with a proper noun. Ding Dongs outrank SnoBalls, while generic cookies are at the rock bottom. By arranging desserts in a pecking order, Nguyen suggests to the reader that if you are judged by what you eat, you want something in the higher tier.

Depending on the level of the students or their skill at "show, don't tell" writing, it might be worth the time to play around with proper nouns and to use them to create an effect. Students can mimic Nguyen's hierarchy by picking a snack food and creating a status list, beginning, for example, "Beneath the status of Ranch Flavored Doritos are . . ."

Another exercise that brings home the power of proper nouns is a T-chart like the one in Figure 2.4. You and/or your students can supply the common nouns, particularly ones that show up in students' writings. For added punch, be sure to share the corresponding proper nouns after stu-dents have filled in the chart.

Figure 2.4. An Exercise for Writing with Specifics

Common Noun	Proper Noun
Grocery store	
Dessert	
Drink	
School	
Friend	
Fast food	
Potato chips	

"Show Don't Tell" Prompt

Both Lamott and Nguyen point out that school lunches have their own code, a right way of doing things and a wrong way of doing things. Describe what you ate for lunch at school when you were younger, whether you brought your lunch or bought it, and how it resembled or did not resemble the lunches of your classmates. If there were social pressures around what to eat at lunchtime, what were they, and how did you handle them? If you prefer, you may write about school lunches as you experience them right now.

Thoughts on Lesson Design

This is another try-it-on writing assignment. Remember that a second practice session like this one is optional. Its purpose is to give students one more chance to rehearse what they have learned about writing with specifics, and to identify and name the strategies they and their peers have used. Time permitting, students can display their papers on a document camera, and/or read their papers aloud and get responses from a small group of classmates or from the entire class. At the least, students can trade papers and highlight or underline the "showing" details. When student writing is spotlighted and analyzed in class, teachers need not scrutinize the papers again in isolation. The real learning occurs in the classroom exchange.

Alternatives to writing about school lunches are other situations where social pressures come into play: recess, assemblies, riding the bus, field trips, group projects, gym class, and so on. The intent is the same: to give students additional practice with strategies such as those listed in Figure 2.5.

Figure 2.5. Strategies for Writing with Specifics

Appropriate adjectives
Active verbs
Intentional and selective description
Bestowing human powers to inanimate objects
Specific details
Comparing one thing to another
Purposeful actions
Examples/illustrations
Elaboration
Re-creating an experience so that the reader lives through it
Proper nouns
Showing contrasts
Creating definitions by describing what something is and isn't
Characterizations
Showing cause and effect
Meaningful dialogue
Revealing a character's inner thoughts

FINAL READING ASSIGNMENT

Mentor Text: *For You Mom, Finally*

The excerpt below describes an incident in the author's life when her mother improvised a questionable snack for a meeting of a young group of Brownies. After reading about the snack, you may find it hard to believe that Ruth Reichl became an expert on food, a well-known food writer, and the editor of a popular food magazine.

Students need to know that Brownies are girls in Grades 2 and 3 who meet regularly, most often after school. They are the youngest group of Girl Scouts, and like their older counterparts, they join for fun and friendship, for building character, and for contributing to their communities.

"Hurry up, hurry up," my mother is shouting as she races through our small apartment, "we're going to be late again!"

This is nothing new; my mother is incapable of arriving anywhere on time. But she has just become the leader of my Brownie troop, and the powers that be have emphasized the importance of punctuality. She grabs a red hat, crams it onto her head, and dashes for the door. I am right behind her. Just as the door begins to close Mom shouts, "Oh, no, I forgot the snack!"

"Mom," I moan. "You can't forget the snack again. You forgot it last week."

"Don't be fresh!" she snaps, inserting herself into the arc of the closing door. "We have no time to shop. Come back in and help me find something delicious."

"We don't have anything," I say flatly.

"Nonsense," she says, striding to the refrigerator.

She surveys the contents with a gimlet eye and gingerly extracts a bowl. It is covered with bright blue fuzz, but she carefully scrapes this off, murmuring, "This must be that chocolate pudding I made last month." She pokes in a finger, tastes tentatively and says triumphantly, "What a good start!"

"There's not very much," I say hopefully. I am aware that any mention of the pudding's antique character will be unwelcome; my mother is a firm believer in the benign nature of mold. "It's not enough for all of us."

"I know that!" she says crossly. "We're going to stretch it. See what you can find in the cupboard."

"Like what?" I ask dubiously.

"Oh, use your imagination," she snaps.

I climb onto the stove so I can reach the cupboard, give the door, which sticks a bit, a firm yank and peer inside. I pull out a box of pretzels, a few prunes, a bag of very stale marshmallows and a jar of strawberry jam. "Perfect!" says Mom. "Hand them down here. Anything else?"

Feeling it would be unwise to mention the sardines or the tin of liver pâté, I pass on to the can of peaches. "Good," says Mom, "give me that too."

As I watch, Mom mixes the jam into the not very moldy chocolate pudding and adds the prunes. "Break those pretzels into little pieces," she commands, "while I chop up the marshmallows and slice the peaches. This is going to be delicious!"

Three minutes later she is wiping her hands. "Let's go," she says.

"Aren't you taking plates?" I ask. "We can't just use our fingers."

Mom sticks a dozen soupspoons in her pocket and cries merrily, "The girls will think it's such fun to eat right out of the bowl!"

I am dubious about this, but to my surprise, they do. While my best friend, Jeanie, and I stick our spoons ostentatiously in and out, consuming nothing, the rest of the girls happily gobble up the goop. "Mrs. Reichl," says Nancy Feld, a dreadful little toady of a child, "you're such a wonderful cook. Could you give the recipe to my mother?"

Mom rewards her with a queenly smile. "Call me Mim, dear," she says, "but I couldn't do that; the recipe is an old family secret." And then she turns to me and whispers triumphantly, "See, I told you. A little mold never hurt anyone!"

I've got Mim Tales by the dozen, and I've used them for years to entertain my friends. As a writer I've always known how lucky I was to have so much material, and my first book opened with Mom accidentally poisoning a couple of dozen people at a party. After the book was published people kept asking, "Did she really do those things?". . .

Then last year, on what would have been her hundredth birthday, I sat down to write one of those speeches in which people traditionally thank their mothers. I scribbled words unthinkingly, but when I looked down at the page I found that I had written something like a Mim Tale. But this was in a different voice, more hers than mine, and it was finally telling her side of the story. . . .

"My mother would have been one hundred years old today," the speech began. "And so I've been thinking about her, and how she helped me to become the person that I am." (Reichl, 2010, pp. 1–7)

Thoughts on Lesson Design

As with previous texts, this one provides a model of "show, don't tell" writing. The stand-out technique is dialogue. But from the work they have done before, students can also identify other techniques Reichl uses to bring the reader into the scene (specific descriptions, active verbs, and so on).

Even before talking about craft, however, students might confer on what the incident is about. To what extent is it about food? About the young girl's relationship with her mother? About the mother's idiosyncratic approach to life and food? How are the writer's adult feelings about her mother different from her feelings as a child?

Integrating Vocabulary

While entertaining, Reichl's piece throws a few curve balls at the reader, particularly in terms of vocabulary. The CCSS call for students to read increasingly complex texts. That means that students and even teachers will run across difficult and unfamiliar words and phrases, among other tough features. Which one of us can whip out a definition for the phrase "gimlet eye" in Reichl's sentence: "'Nonsense,' she says, striding to the refrigerator. She surveys the contents with a gimlet eye and gingerly extracts a bowl"?

Or maybe you remember that "gimlet eye" is a sharp or piercing look or glance? Did you also know that around the year 1420 a gimlet was a small, sharp, woodworking tool?

So that students, particularly ELLs, don't come to a screeching halt when they run across phrases like "gimlet eye," we recommend an activity that comes from *Reading for Understanding* (Shoenbach, Greenleaf, Cziko, & Hurwitz, 1999). Students work in groups to identify *survival words*— "words a reader would have to know in order to have his or her comprehension survive while reading a particular text" (p. 106). In the spirit of inquiry and collaboration, they compare notes and share with each other the meanings of the survival words about which they are most confident. The teacher answers questions, gives additional information, or sends them to other resources like print or online dictionaries.

Focusing on survival words offers significant advantages. Students learn that they don't have to know every word in order to understand what they are reading. They learn when to turn to other readers or dictionaries when they do need to clarify a word. And they become more comfortable with partial knowledge:

> Like comprehension itself, word knowledge is not an all or nothing proposition. As all readers know from their own experience, readers are often somewhat familiar with a word, even if they cannot define it specifically. Similarly, even when they do not have prior knowledge of a word, they may be able to derive its meaning from context. (Shoenbach et al., 1999, p. 106)

We worked in a high school years ago where all the 11th-graders memorized what were known as "SAT words"—25 of them a week, listed randomly. No one seemed to know where the words came from or how they specifically related to the SAT test. Undoubtedly, the lists and the relentless system of weekly ingestion were someone's best guess about test preparation. However, the originator(s) of the list may not have read the research that shows students learn and remember vocabulary best when the words relate to each other and/or to the same general topic or idea.

> Vocabulary instruction should make sense in the context of the reading [or writing] lesson. Words that are related to the selection, the content, or to a thematic unit have instructional potential and should be considered high on the list of candidates for explicit instruction. (Hiebert & Kamil, 2009, p. 12)

FINAL WRITING ASSIGNMENT

Writing Situation. Ruth Reichl writes about an incident in her life that illustrates her mother's approach to food (a little mold never hurt anyone) and her mother's zany character. While the incident is funny, it comes with a lesson learned: an appreciation of her mother.

Writing Directions. Write about a memorable incident in your past when food played some kind of role. The incident should be a moment in time—an hour, or a day or two, not an extended episode over days and weeks. It may or may not involve another person. Remember to use "showing" strategies. Your purpose is to bring your experience to life for an audience of classmates.

Alternative Writing Assignments

The most wide-open alternative assignment is to let students select and write about any incident that stands out for them for some reason. In this case, the bare minimum guidelines are that the students understand the audience and purpose and that they focus on an event that takes place in a short period of time (as opposed to an event that drags on endlessly, like a trip to Disney World). And of course they will want to show the reader what happened in such a way that the reader can visualize the incident and understand its significance.

A less wide-open alternative that connects more closely to the reading is to ask students to write about a time when they were embarrassed, or like Reichl, were afraid they would be embarrassed.

Whichever alternative you or your students choose, this final task rounds out the craft workshops by asking students to make use of the strategies they've learned as they draft and revise.

Revising with Peer Response Groups

Peer response groups bring together several of the big ideas in the CCSS:

- Integration of reading, writing, speaking, and listening
- Collaboration
- Writing as a process, including planning, revising, editing, and rewriting
- Analysis of texts/evaluation of content

Teachers who set up small-group collaboration in their classrooms know the importance of providing clear guidelines and of modeling—not just once but on numerous occasions during the year, especially as the task changes.

For this writing assignment, the goal is for students to read their drafts to an audience of peers to get feedback that will help them improve their second draft by writing with more specifics. Rebekah Caplan (n. d.) explains the process she uses to put the emphasis on "showing" writing:

> I reinforce the awareness of showing and not telling . . . by having students practice spotting telling statements in each others' writings. . . . I ask the students to try and find any sentences that need more information and underline them. Beside that sentence, they are to write the word "show.". . . Every student is being trained to look for non-specificness in each other's writing. They are learning effective criticism. (p. 12)

Ideally, students would be able to make their notations on a computer draft through a web-based program like Google Docs. If not, hard copies work, and when those are not possible, students can read their drafts aloud while their listeners take notes without the benefit of seeing the draft. However you do it, reading drafts aloud is a key component because it helps the author hear his/her voice and catch things that have slipped by; as for the listeners, they get practice in one of life's most challenging activities—paying attention.

Student responders can certainly ask questions about a peer's draft or make other kinds of recommendations. The trick is to teach them ahead of time what constitutes a helpful response. For this purpose, teachers often conduct an actual student response group while other students look on, and then ask everyone to note what they have seen. Another teaching tool is to play with the size of the group. Starting with partners often simplifies the dynamics as students are learning to talk about and analyze each other's writing. Teachers can add to the mix as students become more proficient and competent, from duets to triads, to quartets, and so on.

One other consideration about peer response groups: When teachers gather under the auspices of the Writing Project, they often express their dismay at students' talent for going merrily off task. We suggest keeping the time for response short, especially in the beginning. Let the pressure of the clock do its magic to focus students on the task at hand.

A final note: Students are not limited to peers for responses to their drafts. Teachers can ask students to find one or more adults (parent, school counselor, teacher, coach, custodian, adult relative, neighbor, and so on) to read and comment. In this instance, it's a good idea to provide the adult with the assignment along with questions or guidelines for response.

A Mini Craft Workshop During Revision

The ultimate moment for teaching students is during the revision process.

Timing is everything. When students have something on the page with which to work and motivation to make the writing better, they can be amazingly receptive to a short lesson. It might be a workshop that revisits or reinforces an earlier lesson, for example, "show, don't tell," or one that introduces something new. For the purposes of our lesson design, we chose a workshop on writing conclusions because they frustrate even the most experienced authors.

If you choose to focus on conclusions, you might remind students of some conclusions they have written in the past. In their elementary school years they probably concluded most stories with the words "THE END." Life was easier in those days, because a young writer could put "THE END" anywhere at any time, when the hand got tired or the brain wore out.

At some point most students learn to end a paper by summarizing—a strategy that makes sense in some instances, but not as a steady diet. The problem with the summary is that it can be boring and disappointing. The reader already knows what happened, or in the case of an opinion piece, the reasons for the student writer's point of view. So why subject the reader to more of the same? Is there an alternative, a more satisfying way to end a story?

Yes, and it's harder. What the reader wants to know is the *significance* or the "so what," for example:

- What did the writer learn from the event or experience?
- How did the writer feel about the experience—then or now?
- How did the event or experience change or affect the writer's life?
- What does the writer want the reader to take away from the story?

For this workshop, it's best to use a piece of writing from one of your students' drafts—either as a model or a work in progress to which class members can contribute. In the absence of immediate student writing, professional models will certainly do. Here we show 9th-grader Danielle Decesare's conclusion to her narrative. The gist of the story is that the writer needed to have a blood test, but was terrified of needles. Ultimately, the writer manages to get through the ordeal. She concludes:

> I ambled up out of the chair and out to the waiting room. I was careful not to move my arm, afraid of potential pain. Looking down at my arm I felt proud and accomplished. The feeling sent excitement through my body, like a soldier who'd made it back to base, or a hero that had survived and defeated the villain. There's something about facing your fears that's rewarding and makes you feel triumphant. I felt like I could face the world at this point, just as soon as I took a nap. My breathing had begun to even out, my muscles relaxed, and I couldn't wait to get out of there. It may have been just a usual day to everyone working in the lab, just another 6 vials of blood, but to me I had just conquered my biggest fear. That in itself was worth the prick in my arm.

Notice how the author provides meaning and significance to her experience in the blood lab. She has conquered a personal enemy and uses soldier and hero metaphors to show the magnitude of her triumph. This is a life-changing event, but she also treats it with some humor ("just as soon as I took a nap") and gives it perspective ("it was just a usual day to everyone working in the lab").

One more thought: This workshop emphasizes reflective conclusions, and while there are other ways to conclude personal narratives, the benefit of teaching reflective conclusions is that they have some transferability to informational and argumentative writing, where it is also important to zero in on significance.

The Party's Over . . . Or Is It?

So now we have come full circle with a lesson design for narrative writing, one that incorporates reading, writing, speaking, and listening. Except for the grand finale, which is sometimes not so grand.

> In the writing workshop the student learns, sometimes slowly and painfully, how to make meaning clear. Students are always surprised that what they think is fully developed and clear to them is so difficult for others to understand. (Murray, 1985, p. 189)

Too often, final drafts die a slow agonizing death that looks something like this. The teacher ruins his or her social life grading the final drafts and writing laborious comments. The students read the grade, complain, skim the comments, complain, compare results, complain, and then put the paper to permanent rest.

Something must be done! Several years ago, during a Bay Area Writing Project (BAWP) summer institute, several of the participants (composition instructors at UC Berkeley) noted that the idea that inspired them most over the 5 weeks came from a 1st-grade teacher named Kathy. "How could that be?" the director asked, alluding to the many years that separate 1st grade from the 1st year of college. "Exactly what inspired you?" "She celebrates the kids' writing when it's done," said one of the college instructors. "It just never occurred to us that there is something to be celebrated. We are pretty cut and dried—tell the student what passes and what needs fixing. Not much tipping of the hat when it comes to recognizing effort or accomplishment."

Here are some of the "celebration" suggestions from Kathy and her BAWP colleagues: Enlarge the audience for the finished product. Take time for a read-around or an author's chair. Invite students to read a certain number of their peers' papers and write post-it comments, either online or on print copies. Appoint several students to assemble an e-anthology.

And to help both the teacher and student deal with evaluating the final draft, ask students to write an afterword—a short reflection on how they wrote the paper, where they got their ideas, what came together easily, what was hard, what worked, what didn't. Consider commenting only on the afterword. That's where students have consolidated their learning.

CLASSROOM EXAMPLES: LESSON DESIGN IN ACTION

We look now at how two teachers use design elements such as starters, workshops and models, try-it-on writings, longer polished pieces, feedback and revision, and finally, celebration. In both of these cases, the teachers share their own writing as models of what's possible. In the first case, a high school teacher makes notebooks the jumping off place for students to learn sophisticated narrative techniques. In the second, a middle school example, vocabulary building is a key ingredient for ELL students.

Case Study: Learning About Narrative Strategies

Brendan Nelson teaches English at a suburban high school in Danville, California. His 9th-graders spend 6 weeks digging into narrative writing. Nelson has his own version of "showing" writing: interspersing the action with thoughts and feelings. He observes that "the kids' idea of narrative is limited to describing what happened. I try to get them to go into greater depth" (all Nelson quotes are from a personal communication, July 29, 2013).

Prewriting. Nelson begins by sharing his own writing with his students. "I write a short narrative that's just description and then one that includes introspection. We read a lot of narratives or parts of narratives. Then I get them to write. After they have been writing for a while, they sit with a partner and read what they have. They underline areas where they need to 'explode the moment' by slowing down and getting into their feelings."

Nelson does not skimp on time for students to rehearse before they take on a big piece of writing. "I have them practice telling their story to a partner. Together they write down questions at various points in the telling: what was going on and what was in the person's mind?" Student writing also serves as a teaching model. Nelson notes, "We look at one piece of student writing on a document camera and we ask questions as a class—how do we get into the person's thoughts?"

Before attempting a rough draft, students write smaller narratives in their writer's notebooks, finding events they like to write about. They also create timelines: On the top of the timeline they note what happened. On the bottom they jot down what

Teacher and author Barry Lane popularized the term *explode the moment.* On his YouTube videos, he shows students how to slow down the pace and explode a moment across an entire page "so the reader can feel what you felt and see what you saw." (Lane, 2007)

Author Barry Lane used the term *thoughtshot* to describe a look at what a person is thinking and feeling. According to Lane, thoughtshots "place events in a context and give the reader and the writer a reason to be interested. 'It was my first night on the job as a pizza delivery man and I had a feeling it might be my last.'" (1993, p. 44) they were thinking and feeling at each moment of the event (walking up to the gym, the walk into the gym, looking up on the stage, and so on).

According to Nelson, the purpose of the timeline is for students to "practice developing the important, useful tools that any good personal narrative writer uses, including vivid description, engaging narrative, thoughtful exploration of thoughts and feelings, effective use of back story/background information, etc."

When students construct their timelines, Nelson tells them: "Arrange your events chronologically, from beginning to end. On the first part of the timeline, jot down what happens. Below that, jot down your thoughts, feelings, predictions, reactions, misgivings, etc. Therefore, the top part will pertain to factual events, while the bottom part will examine your mental and psychological landscape." Figure 2.6 illustrates this process.

This kind of front-loading pays off for students as they approach the task of writing a full-blown narrative. As shown in Figure 2.7, Nelson frames their assignment to capitalize on the weeks of modeling and practicing.

Figure 2.6. A Timeline Linking External Events and Internal Reactions

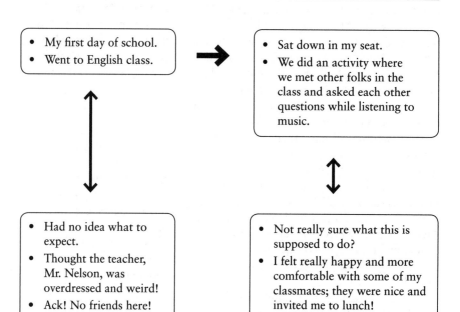

At this point, students do much of their work in the computer lab, including their feedback to each other. Again Nelson models what he wants the students to do when they read and respond to each other's drafts: point out places where the writer can elaborate more on thoughts and feelings, where to beef up descriptions or insert meaningful dialogue. Students cycle once more through what they've learned and how to best put it into their narratives. They pay attention to the old writer's nemesis: how to write a conclusion that packs a punch; how to reflect back on an experience and capture its significance—what does it mean to the writer now?

The narrative unit ends on a high note. Nelson conducts a publication celebration that includes an author's chair. Students read the parts of their narratives that they are most proud of, and of course everyone claps as classmates say what they liked. Some papers make it to the wall, and all of them get saved. They are well worth saving.

Student Writing. Here are some excerpts from a 9th-grader's paper. Note the way the author weaves together action, thoughts, and feelings.

Figure 2.7. Assignment for a Polished Piece of Writing

Your Life, Your Story: A Personal Narrative

Looking back on the entries in your writer's notebook, select one of those entries (or, if you wish, devise a new topic) on which to write a personal narrative. A *personal narrative* is a detailed, specific account of an event that happened to you and your thoughts and feelings during significant parts of the event.

When selecting a topic for your personal narrative, consider the following criteria:

1. The event should be significant to you, and you should enjoy writing about it.
2. The event should allow you to explore your thoughts and feelings about certain moments in great detail.
3. The event should contain enough details to allow you to write about it in 3–5 pages.
4. The event should not be too broad in scope (i.e., do not write about your trip to Italy but a particular part of that trip).

Please make sure that your paper addresses the following points, in addition to the criteria above:

1. Reveal your thoughts and emotions as you describe significant parts of the event; allow the reader to get inside your head and see the event through your eyes.
2. Include detailed, focused descriptions of the setting, people, and other important aspects of the event.
3. Remember, this should not be simply a description of events, but a thoughtful depiction of what happened and what was going on in your mind as the event was unfolding.

Oh Say Can You Sing?

By Abbey Watson

Almost four years ago, I was approached by my softball coach after a long, sweat, dirt, and blood-filled tournament. She explained that she had connections with the coordinator of an upcoming baseball tournament, and he was in search of a singer willing to sing the National Anthem at the start of the tournament. My heart leapt with excitement. I immediately pictured famous singers on TV singing at football games and baseball games and how I always wanted to do that. Thrilled at the opportunity, I agreed without thinking twice. . . .

> Para. 1. Sets the scene. Orients the reader. Signals the reader that this opportunity is a big deal.

The day of the tournament, I woke up to a sickening surprise: my throat felt like it was being rubbed against sandpaper. When I felt pain while swallowing, my stomach dropped to the floor, and my hopes and courage dropped along with it. I was worried I wouldn't be able to sing to the best of my ability in this condition, but I knew I didn't have a choice. I thought of disappointing my coach, and I worried the coordinator would think I was unreliable. There was no way I could back out at this point, and part of me knew I couldn't give up such an incredible opportunity.

> Para. 2. Builds tension by describing sandpaper throat and plummeting confidence.

My stomach was an acrobat, flipping every which way as I arrived at the field. All I could see for miles were people. Brothers, sisters, parents, aunts, uncles, cousins, grandparents, all of which would hear me sing in t-minus-twenty minutes. My own brother, sister, mom, dad, grandma, and grandpa, and I piled out of the car. I walked ahead with my mom to find the coordinator, who greeted me with a big, whitened smile and told me where to meet him in about fifteen minutes. I knew that this fifteen minutes would not be like the fifteen minutes left of the very last class before the weekend that passes dreadfully slow because you're eager to get out of school, but more like the fifteen minutes left before you need to get up in the morning that passes faster than lightening because you want it to last.

> Para. 3. Uses interior monologue to alert the reader that disaster might lie ahead.

"Welcome to our annual All-Star Tournament! To start us off, I am honored to introduce our singer of the National Anthem . . . " The booming voice carried out clearly through the series of baseball fields and captured the attention of everyone in attendance.

It was sunny. I could feel the sun beating down on my back almost as well as I could feel my heart beating in my chest. All I could think about as I walked over to the pitcher's mound was the increasing amount of fear in my belly. *What if I sing the wrong notes?* I thought. *What if I forget the words? What if no one thinks it sounds good?*

Paras. 4 & 5. Slow down the pace ("explode the moment"). Show actions and feelings.

As I walked up to the place where I would momentarily reveal my voice to what seemed to be a never ending sea of people, I felt dizzy as if I had spun around in a circle too many times. With shaking hands, I gingerly accepted the microphone from the coordinator. It felt like a boulder in my weak, sweating hands. Standing on the mound, I felt microscopic compared to the enormous crowd waiting for me to start. I took a deep breath and began to sing the famous words, trying to turn my focus from the terror that was making my chest feel heavy as if there were a weight strapped to it.

Looking at my feet, I continued to sing the words just as I was taught. Feeling a sudden and unexpected burst of courage, I slowly removed my gaze from the ground and transferred it to the hundreds of people watching. Every pair of eyes seemed to be stuck to me with glue, all waiting to see if such a small girl could do such a big song any justice. Their expectations were my worst enemy, but I was prepared for battle.

Paras. 6, 7, & 8. Dramatize emotional ups and downs. Use words of the song to mark progress.

"And the rockets' red glare . . . " I sang cleanly. I hit my first big note in the song with clarity and confidence. Doing so, I heard a few distant cheers. They may have seemed insignificant and unnoticeable to others, but they boosted my courage and gave me the initiative I needed to continue singing well. With the words "banner yet wave," I felt that same terror sneaking stealthily back into my belly, but I pushed it away as quickly as it crept in, because I knew that second-guessing myself would only make matters worse. I continued singing, beginning to get lost in a place only I knew. I focused so much on the words and sang them out with the strength that such powerful words deserved. All of my worries, stresses, and fears seemed to temporarily leave me as I became more and more lost in the song.

Paras. 9 & 10. Answer the question "so what?" Why is this a significant event?

"O'er the land of the free!" I sang with all of the power I could muster. I heard cheers and fought the smile that was slowly creeping onto my face. With the last few words of the song, I felt my heart race with adrenaline. I felt so many different emotions consuming me internally and I was not sure whether to laugh or to cry. I was not even finished holding the last note when I heard clapping and cheering.

I had finished the song, but even more so, conquered my fear. I felt a wave of relief crash over me and wash away all of my doubts as I walked off of the mound and over to my family who greeted me with hugs and kisses. I knew I had accomplished something very difficult and I was proud of myself for doing so. The smiles on their faces told me they were proud of me as well.

Not only did I grow as a singer through that experience, but I also grew as a person. I felt braver and more confident. I no longer get that nervous when singing in front of large crowds, and I've learned to take as many kinds of opportunities as I can. Even though most people might not remember that tournament, it is forever engraved in my memory as a life-changing experience.

Case Study: Setting the Stage for Narrative Writing with English Language Learners

Eighth graders in Zack Lewis-Murphy's English companion class share one thing in common: They need a lot of extra support in learning to read and write. What they don't share are similar backgrounds. The class is a medley of languages, cultures, and abilities, with almost half the students learning English as a second language. "The subject of food is a good common denominator for these kids," says Lewis-Murphy, a 10-year veteran. "When we went around the class talking about favorite foods, the exchange was so positive. As we know, kids can be very harsh with each other. But in this case, they expressed something about their culture and got support from other students. Plus they know the subject matter well. Among the girls, many said they have been cooking all their lives" (all Lewis-Murphy quotes are from a personal communication, October 14, 2013).

The San Leandro, California, middle school where Lewis-Murphy teaches is a Title I–funded school that failed in the past to make Adequate Yearly Progress (AYP). While teachers work from pacing guides, they also work overtime to reach and engage their students. Lewis-Murphy prefaces his units of study by showing students his own writing and by using it to demonstrate designated skills. Personal pronouns are difficult for some of his ELL students, notes Lewis-Murphy, and all the students need help in remembering how to write dialogue, right down to the basics of giving each speaker a separate line. That's where a teacher model can start the ball rolling.

Mentor Text: "My First Attempt at Cooking"

Lewis-Murphy uses his own writing (excerpted here) for lessons on description, dialogue, and first-person point of view:

My family and I sat around the dinner table as I grumbled about the quality of food. I was 11 years old and already tired of my mom's cooking. It seemed to me that we had the same redundant variations of meals continuously. I would always find fault with my mom's food and verbalize it to her on a consistent basis. One night as I made snide comments about her cooking, she reached her breaking point.

"You don't like my cooking, fine," she said annoyed. "You're cooking tomorrow night and we'll see how you do."

"Fine," I said, not knowing what I was getting myself into.

After school the next day, my mom took me to the grocery store. She would buy anything for me to cook that night. There were only two parameters she gave me: I could not buy anything premade and there had to be a vegetable in the meal. I took the shopping cart around the grocery store, feeling grown. I grabbed the needed ingredients and my mom paid for the groceries. My first lesson in cooking was to begin.

We got home at 5:00 pm and my mom informed me that the meal had to be ready by 6:30 pm, right when my dad got home. Plenty of time I thought. Even though I used the same kitchen my entire life, I realized that I did not know where half of the cooking supplies were located. I opened and closed cabinets, looking for a pot that was the right size or a cutting board. Fifteen minutes of searching went by and I had not even started cooking. A sense of panic began to rise in me.

Realizing time was slipping away, I decided to lay out all the groceries on the tile cabinet and begin preparations. Since the chicken was the main feature of my meal, I thought I should properly prepare the chicken. It took a good 20 minutes of sticking my fingers inside to remove the fat from the chicken. I then took BBQ sauce and marinated the chicken, but I poured too much, with the sauce spreading all over the chicken and pan. The chicken was ready to cook, but I realized I had forgotten to pre-heat the oven. Although the oven was supposed to be set at 375 degrees, I raised the temperature to 475 because I forgot to pre-heat.

Next came the cornbread. I mixed the necessary ingredients and stirred the batter numerous times. I then smoothed the batter onto the baking sheet and threw it in the oven with the chicken, forgetting that I had raised the temperature to 475 degrees.

Next came the salad. I rinsed the lettuce and tomatoes and began cutting the tomatoes. It was now 6:30 and dinner was still not ready. Just then, my nose detected smoke in the air. I looked over at the oven and smoke was billowing out of there. I frantically opened the stove and saw that the BBQ sauce was burning on the baking sheet. Just then, my mom came in and told me it was 6:30 and dinner should be ready now. Tension filled my body as I peeled the crispy chicken off the pan. Black skin from the burnt chicken flaked off. I then cut into the cornbread and realized with dread that even though the crust was burned, the inside was under cooked and still sopping wet. I was in a full panic.

It was now 6:45 and my brother and sister were complaining that they were hungry.

"Is it ready yet?" they said in unison.

"In one second," I yelled at them.

I had no choice. Dinner had to be served. With sweat pouring down my forehead, I dished the food and served it to my family. The chicken was burnt. Flaky, charbroiled skin could be peeled off the meat. The cornbread was hard on the crust, but soupy on the inside. It was almost inedible. Even the tossed salad was sloppy and wet. The meal was a total disaster and I knew it. My grand vision of a spectacular meal was ruined by the reality of cooking. My sister complained that her chicken was burnt and crispy.

"Oh, just eat your food," I snapped at her.

My mom sat there with a big smile on her face.

After that day, I complained less often about my mom's cooking. I just knew I didn't want to cook anymore.

Once his students have inspected Lewis-Murphy's piece, they read other professional models and talk through them. Conversation plays a big role in a class with so many ELL students, according to Lewis-Murphy. Every exercise, every quick write, every short lesson begins and ends with students talking in pairs, small groups, or as a class. When they actually sit down to draft their own pieces, they have accumulated content and vocabulary for the task at hand.

Building Vocabulary. A significant challenge for Lewis-Murphy is expanding the vocabulary of English language learners who may or may not be fascinated by new words, especially when they encounter them in fifth period, right after lunch. There is certainly no shortage of words to be learned. For the forthcoming assignment Lewis-Murphy located words about food on the Internet and made up a list for his students—everything from *lip-smacking* to *crunchy* to *tantalizing*. Once students had done a quick write on a favorite food, Lewis-Murphy gave out the word list. Students read through it aloud in pairs, talking about the words as they went. And then came the all-important practice when the students rewrote their quick writes, trying out words that would add zest and flavor. Even more words showed up when they wrote their longer pieces about cooking a meal or encountering a new food. Lewis-Murphy notes that the words had meaning because they pertained to a specific topic and because the students had time to play with and practice them.

Assignment for a First Draft. Lewis-Murphy gives his students a choice of three topics:

1. The first time you tried a food you really enjoyed or hated. Describe the experience.

2. The first time you cooked a meal. Describe the experience, including when and for whom. Be sure to tell how old you were.
3. A meal you remember. Describe what made it special, including who was with you and where you were.

Student Writing. Even in a first draft we find evidence of all the front-loading Lewis-Murphy provided.

The First Time I Made a Meal

By Amian Ajah Brewer

I was nine years old. I had only been helping people cook for 3 years before this day, but today was the day I had to make a meal all by myself. I was kind of nervous because I was under harsh pressure but I had to prove to my grandma that I was a great cook. (Since I had bragged about it since I was 4 years old).

That day, I cooked an appetizing steak, and a very cheesy bowl of macaroni and cheese. (with a little help from my family) My family was underestimating me the WHOLE TIME.

"You can't do that!" said Lyric (my sister).

"Your never going to make that" said Mom.

"I bet it's going to taste horrible" said Cavasy (my brother).

But it didn't phase me. I started to pour the ingrediants into the pot to prepare the macaroni, then, I turned on the stove for the steak while my grandmother helped season the steak and marinade it with barbeque sauce.

Then I put the steak in the oven and the macaroni on the stove and turned it on 350 degrees so it could start cooking.

About 30 minutes later I went to check on my macaroni when I see it boiling over in water like an erupting volcano. Luckily, nobody was in the house at the time, so I just cut it down. Then I checked on my steak. It was starting to cook but I could see that it looked tasteful and it was with a high temper. I then went to sit back down and relax for another 20 minutes.

When that 20 minutes was over, I was starting to smell the "southern style" steak and could almost taste the tenderness on my tongue. It was so yummy!

Anyways, I checked my macaroni too, and I observed it needed just a little more cheese, so I added a little more cheese and took it out of the pot and put it in a big orange bowl. Then I had to put a little bit more seasoning on the steak, it was missing something. It was missing garlic! I sprinkled the garlic lightly on the steak.

I was beginning to smell the steak a lot more, so, I took it out the oven and set it on the top of the stove. I took out plates for everyone and put the macaroni and steak on each plate & served it to everyone.

When I passed it around to everybody I guess they changed their minds, because they then were saying in unison: "This tastes so good, Amian you did so good."

With everybodys mouths full of food, they were laughing and making jokes and having a good time.

I guess I made a good meal this time.

Clearly this student writer has picked up on the very things Lewis-Murphy intended when he wrote and shared his own writing, and then used it as a teaching tool. She has included specific descriptions and meaningful dialogue and has demonstrated control of first-person point of view. She has also used the teacher's model as a jumping-off place for her own story, in both its content and organization.

For this small unit of study, Lewis-Murphy did not ask his students to revise and edit their drafts. However, peer response gets its due in Lewis-Murphy's schema. "It creates a community within a classroom and gives kids an audience beyond the teacher. A lot of middle school is about 'no one understands me.' Reading each other's papers offers shared experiences. The conversation I want kids to have is to say the positive first. What did you like about this paper? Then if we are working on dialogue or descriptive language, I want the students to make the suggestions. When peers say it, it's so much better than if the teacher says it, but it also adds validity to teacher comments."

Lewis-Murphy sees peer response not as a magic bullet, but as a huge force for good in the classroom: "It creates relationships within the classroom. It builds communication around an academic subject, and it actually enhances openness in writing and deepens it."

Students Weigh In. Not to be forgotten is student motivation—a huge concern for Lewis-Murphy. It's important that his students find assignments relevant and accessible. So how did this one fare on the student barometer? In answering the questions, "Did you enjoy writing about your favorite food? Was this a good topic for you?" most students responded positively:

> "It was easy to write about food."
>
> "I loved talking about my favorite food and it was a good topic to discuss my culture."
>
> "I love food."
>
> "It was okay."
>
> "It was a modern and interesting topic to write about."

In answering the question, "Do you think the topic made a difference to your having things to write about?" most students indicated that the topic of food was accessible:

"Yes, because it was a lot easier to write about food we know a lot about."

"I can talk about food all day."

"I don't think the topic made a difference."

"Yes, because it's better than most things I write about at school."

"Another topic [would be better] because I feel that with food you have to put more detail in the writing."

Students were especially definite about the benefits of the teacher's model writing. Here are some of their answers to the questions, "Did it help you to see your teacher's writing example on the topic? Why?"

"Yes it was. So I would have an idea on what to write about."

"Yes because it gave me a good example."

"It did help me because it showed me the steps."

"Yes because it gave me more ideas on how to start my topic."

"Yes because I then could see what he expected us to write on our memoirs."

"Yes because it mostly showed us what to do or how to do it."

LAST THOUGHTS

In her book *Bird by Bird,* Anne Lamott (1995) underscores the idea that writing is not a solo dance:

> And all the while you are writing away, editing, revising, trying new leads, new endings, until finally, at some point, you want some feedback. You want other people to read it. You want to know what they think. We are social animals, and we are trying to communicate with others of our species, and up to now you have been alone in a hole getting your work done. You have no idea whether it sings to anyone but you. You wouldn't spend a month on an oil painting and then mummify it. You would hang it where people could see it. (pp. 151–152)

While there may be some writers who can just sit down and write, most of us need all the support we can get. A big advantage of setting students in motion to read and write and speak and listen together is that these activities create a community. What happens in a community? People watch out for each other. They share. They invest in each other's well-being and success. A community of writers is no different.

Of course, communities are not built overnight. As teachers, the two of us have found comfort in the idea that we don't have to do everything at once. Just experimenting with a small chunk, such as asking students to talk with partners before and during their writing, starts us on the road to establishing a community. It may be that way for you too. Dive in where it's comfortable.

CHAPTER 3

Extending the Range of Writing

Several years ago Sandy (coauthor Sandra Murphy) went to cooking school on a lark. Although she already knew how to make Sloppy Joes and mac and cheese for starving teenagers, she wanted to know more than how to feed a crowd of nondiscriminating eaters. Within a week of enrolling in the cooking school taught by Sylvie, a teacher from France, Sandy had expanded her repertoire to include elegant dishes such as cantaloupe and avocado salad, stacked omelet harlequin, roast pepper gazpacho, ricotta soufflé, iced tiramisu, and osso bucco. Sylvie was obsessed with using fresh ingredients, but even more important, she wanted her students to become versatile cooks. "When you really know how to cook, you can go into a market, buy what's fresh, and come up with a meal for *un roi* (a king)," she said.

This got us thinking about how many of our secondary students are stuck in the mac and cheese phase of writing. That is, they have a limited repertoire of genres, strategies, and styles. In a single classroom, for example, teachers might work with students who can chronicle a football game in play-by-play detail but not argue successfully for better helmets; students who can nail storytelling but struggle when it comes to explaining a concept; and students who are gifted in writing about a camping trip, yet are novices at using commas and quotation marks. In other words, every writer has strengths in some areas and needs more work in others.

Educational theorists have long argued about the proper progression of the writing continuum and what genres to teach at various grade levels. James Moffett was among those who suggested substantial alternatives to the traditional elementary curriculum of his day—writing about holidays and summer vacations and friendly letters—and to a secondary curriculum focused almost entirely on literary criticism. More recent work in genre theory has added to the understanding that students need to learn many variations in writing for different purposes and audiences and in different contexts (Cope & Kalantzis, 1993; Swales, 1990). In short, they need to get closer to Sylvie's notion of versatility—knowing how to choose the freshest ingredients and how to use them to create an array of satisfying presentations.

When we talk about giving students experiences with a variety of genres or kinds of writing, we are referring to one aspect of *range*. Students who can cozy up to a journal, craft a memoir, explain a process, and argue for a cause have a huge advantage. Their versatility will carry them a long way down the path to success in higher education and careers as well as the path to personal discovery.

In this chapter we focus on how to help students become those versatile writers. Rather than presenting a single lesson design, as we did in Chapter 2, we offer multiple ways of teaching and scaffolding informational and argumentative writing. And in case words like *information* and *argument* evoke visions of student boredom, rest assured that there is good news ahead. Working on these kinds of writing is anything but dull.

CAPTURING THE BIG IDEA OF RANGE

The CCSS call for a variety of purposes, audiences, and tasks, but they also complicate the idea of range. For example, the anchor standards specify that students "Write routinely over extended time frames (time for research, reflection, and revision) and shorter time frames (a single sitting or a day or two)"(CCSSO & NGA, 2010, p. 41). Why ask students to write in a time crunch? While it's true that the Constitution was not written in 50 minutes, students still have to produce impromptu essays for exit exams and timed writing samples for prospective employers as part of the interview process. Colleges still hand out blue books and expect students to show what they know in a couple of hours or less. And bosses won't always wait around for draft three; businesses operate on the fast track, especially in the quick-turnaround era of emails, texts, and tweets. So interspersing opportunities for students to write while the timer runs with longer pieces that have the benefit of multiple responses and revisions has a real-world purpose in addition to meeting the CCSS expectations for range.

The CCSS call on students to write as individuals, but also in collaboration with others. Think about a time when you have written for a public audience, and when you really wanted to get right. Did you write it by yourself? Did you consult with someone on what should go in it? Did you ask a friend to read it before you sent it out? Learning to write individually or collaboratively with others is part of range. Students with experiences at all points on the continuum have an advantage when they enter college and the workplace, where so many projects depend on teamwork.

The concept of range has multiple moving parts. Figure 3.1 presents a summary of this multilayered idea as it is threaded throughout the CCSS.

The word *genre* pops up in the center of Figure 3.1. What is a genre, anyway? A graduation speech is a genre. It has typical themes ("climb every mountain," "the future of the world depends on you") and functional elements (an exhortation to make the world a better place, a motivational metaphor). The speech happens in a specific setting and has certain social

Figure 3.1. What to Look for in a Curriculum That Promotes Range

A variety of writing tasks with a variety of

- Purposes
- Audiences
- Genres

A variety of writing conditions

- With different lengths of time
- With and without collaboration
- With and without scaffolding and support
- With and without technology

---

purposes (recognition, rite of passage, inspiration). Sitting in chairs or bleachers, the audience—parents, grandparents, squirmy siblings, boyfriends, and girlfriends—laugh or pull out handkerchiefs at the appropriate moments.

Another familiar genre is "how to" writing, such as manuals, recipes, directions, and instructions. And don't forget argument. Our world is filled with movie and food reviews, letters to editors, and opinion pieces. Genres make things easier for readers because the form and style signal what's coming. Readers know what to expect. Genres also help writers by providing a conventional arrangement in which to organize and present ideas.

When it comes to the CCSS, however, teachers we've talked to feel uncertain about how the designated types of writing—narrative, information, and argument—play out in real life and in the classroom. What qualifies as informational writing? they ask. Is it the same thing as expository writing? What characterizes an argument? Is there a way to progress from one kind of writing to another? In this chapter about range we concentrate on framing the genres of informational and argumentative writing in a conceptually accessible way. While we continue to comment on lesson design, the focus of this chapter is on understanding two very complex ideas—*range* and *genre*—rather than on fully mapped-out lessons.

Case Study: Learning About Range in a Summer Institute

In 1973 when James Gray and Cap Lavin were planning to inaugurate the Bay Area Writing Project at the University of California–Berkeley, they decided, almost as an afterthought, that the teachers who attended the summer institute should write. As valuable as research and best practices might be, Gray and Lavin reasoned that teachers should also experience what they were preparing to teach others. After all, piano teachers play the piano. Driving teachers drive. Why shouldn't writing teachers know what it means to write?

But what should they write? What combination of assignments would place them in the shoes of their students and, at the same time, expand their own horizons as writers? As Gray (2000) explained in his memoir *Teachers at the Center*, he wanted teachers to have the freedom to choose what to write, yet he also wanted to give them a launching pad should they need one. So he offered a structure that included three major pieces of writing, on a topic of personal choice with no two pieces alike—"an assignment that typically moves the writer from a personal experience to an essay about some idea inherent in the initial experience." This multifaceted assignment, Gray explained, "invites experimentation in genre and point of view and guarantees the writer a varied writing experience, and as such it serves as a model for student writers as well" (p. 85).

Among the many participants who accepted the invitation to write in different ways on a chosen topic was a young teacher named Kimberly who had recently adopted a baby daughter. Her first paper described the experience of completing endless application forms, the agonizing wait for approval, and then finally the moment of meeting her new child. Kimberly's second piece of writing was a letter to her baby daughter, telling her all the reasons why her parents were so eager and elated to adopt her. Kimberly intended to save this letter to give to her daughter during her teenage years, perhaps anticipating the need for bonding at that particularly turbulent time in adolescence. For her last writing piece, Kimberly read widely about adoption, shared the information with her readers, and argued for an easier process for adopting children.

Today there are hundreds of teachers like Kimberly at National Writing Project sites around the country who are trying on new forms or points of view so they can better understand how to convey the structures and applications of writing genres to their students. The genius of Gray's assignment was its direction to write about what matters and then to push its boundaries and test its range. And as it happens in this particular case, the pieces Kimberly wrote fall within the three broad categories of writing identified in the CCSS: narrative, informational, and argumentative. But note that Kimberly was able to choose her topic as well as her purposes, audiences, and genres. In terms of classroom teaching, the invitation to students to experiment is another strategy for expanding their range.

TAKING THE PLUNGE:
INVESTIGATIVE AND INFORMATIONAL WRITING

Investigative writing is a bridge into informational writing.

When it comes to taking the plunge into the deeper, murkier water known as the "harder" kinds of writing, Jim Moffett has some lifesaving advice. First, he acknowledges what most teachers dread, that is, the moment when they must move students from narrative or personal experience writing to a more formal genre. Instead of setting aside a D-Day for cutting off narrative and requiring a thesis-driven essay, Moffett (1989a) recommends building a bridge with the kinds of informational/investigative writing that journalists practice.

> You go look, you go ask, or you go look it up—three main things that reporters and researchers do. They go on site, visit, observe, and take notes. Or they interview one or many people, and again they take notes. Or what they can't get from looking and asking they go look up and see what other people have said about this. They go to records, documents, books and so on. (p. 4)

We call this advice "lifesaving" for several reasons. It captures the idea of writing across a range without having to put boxes around different kinds of writing. One kind of writing can actually support another, and indeed it can flow into and be incorporated into another. And Moffett's advice is also practical: The research/reporting bridge can build content for other uses—an argumentative piece, for example.

Like Moffett, George Hillocks advocates investigative writing, although he calls it "inquiry." In his own investigation of nearly 500 research studies Hillocks (1986) found that the positive effects of an "inquiry" approach to teaching writing—developing enough content to write something worth reading—were significantly greater than other approaches. Focusing on content, Hillocks (2005) says, "gives students the power to work with ideas, far more important than encouraging them to toss random thoughts into a foreordained framework"(p. 243).

Mentor Text: *In Defense of Food*

Michael Pollan (2008) claims that food is actually disappearing from our grocery stores. In its place are food products with unrecognizable ingredients. In the section below, Pollan gives his rules for eating real, ordinary food.

> DON'T EAT ANYTHING YOUR GREAT GRANDMOTHER WOULDN'T RECOGNIZE AS FOOD. Why your great grandmother? Because at this point your mother and possibly even your grandmother is as confused as the rest of us; to be safe we need to go back at least a couple generations, to a time before the advent of most modern foods. So depending on your age (and your grandmother), you may need to go back to your great- or even great-great grandmother. Some nutritionists recommend going back even further. John Yudkin, a British nutritionist whose early alarms about the dangers of refined carbohydrates were overlooked in the 1960s and 1970s, once advised, "just don't eat anything your Neolithic ancestors wouldn't have recognized and you'll be ok."

What would shopping this way mean in the supermarket? Well, imagine your great grandmother at your side as you roll down the aisles [of the supermarket]. You're standing together in front of the dairy case. She picks up a package of Go-Gurt Portable Yogurt tubes—and has no idea what this could possibly be. Is it a food or a toothpaste? And how, exactly, do you introduce it into your body? You could tell her it's just yogurt in a squirtable form, yet if she read the ingredients label she would have every reason to doubt that that was in fact the case. Sure, there's some yogurt in there, but there are also a dozen other things that aren't remotely yogurtlike, ingredients she would probably fail to recognize as foods of any kind, including high-fructose corn syrup, modified corn starch, kosher gelatin, carrageenan, tricalcium phosphate, natural and artificial flavors, vitamins, and so forth. (And there's a whole other list of ingredients for the "berry bubblegum bash" flavoring, containing everything but berries or bubblegum.) How did yogurt, which in your great grandmother's day consisted simply of milk inoculated with a bacterial culture, ever get to be so complicated? Is a product like Go-Gurt Portable Yogurt still a whole food? A food of any kind? Or is it just a food product? . . .

Consider a loaf of bread, one of the "traditional foods that everyone knows." . . . As your grandmother could tell you, bread is traditionally made using a remarkably small number of familiar ingredients: flour, yeast, water, and a pinch of salt will do it. But industrial bread—even industrial whole-grain bread—has become a far more complicated product of modern food science (not to mention commerce and hope). Here's the complete ingredients list for Sara Lee's Soft & Smooth Whole Grain White Bread. (Wait a minute—isn't "Whole Grain White Bread" a contradiction in terms? Evidently not anymore.)

Enriched bleached flour [wheat flour, malted barley flour, niacin, iron, thiamin mononitrate (vitamin B_1), riboflavin (vitamin B_2), folic acid], water, whole grains [whole wheat flour, brown rice flour (rice flour, rice bran)], high fructose corn syrup [hello!], whey, wheat gluten, yeast, cellulose. Contains 2% or less of each of the following: honey, calcium sulfate, vegetable oil (soybean and/or cottonseed oils), salt, butter (cream, salt), dough conditioners (may contain one or more of the following: mono- and diglycerides, ethoxylated mono- and diglycerides, ascorbic acid, enzymes, azodicarbonamide), guar gum, calcium propionate (preservative), distilled vinegar, yeast nutrients (monocalcium phosphate, calcium sulfate, ammonium sulfate), corn starch, natural flavor, beta carotene (color), vitamin D_3, soy lecithin, soy flour.

There are many things you could say about this intricate loaf of "bread," but note first that even if it managed to slip by your great grandmother (because it *is* a loaf of bread, or at least is called one and strongly resembles one), the product fails every test proposed under rule number two: It's got unfamiliar ingredients (monoglycerides I've heard of before, but ethoxylated monoglyceriedes?); unpronounceable ingredients (try "azodicarbonamide"); it exceeds the maximum of five ingredients (by roughly thirty-six); and it contains high-fructose corn syrup. Sorry, Sara Lee, but your Soft & Smooth Whole Grain White Bread is not food and if not for the indulgence of the FDA could not even be labeled "bread." (pp. 148–152)

Investigative Writing Prompt

Select a food you eat and also suspect might horrify your great-grandmother (or your great-grandfather) with its "modern" ingredients. Investigate the ingredients of the food, either by reading the actual food label or looking online. Find out as much as you can about the nature of these ingredients and how they affect your health. Write a letter to your great-grandmother, giving her this information, and explaining why and under what circumstances you eat this food.

Thoughts on Lesson Design

In transitional assignments like this one, students experience a range of literacy activities: writing in connection with reading and research, writing to provide information to a particular audience, and writing that moves students from one genre to another.

Investigative writing has another advantage. Rather than asking students to slam the door on one kind of writing and crank open another, perhaps more foreboding door, transitional writing invites them to look through both doors at once. They can blend their own experiences and observations with the information that comes from their research. Thus one genre plays off the other.

Moving from Investigation to Information

Have you ever been buttonholed at a party by someone eager to give you a lot of information on a subject that is of no interest to you? The air is filled with words that serve no apparent social purpose. You are at a loss for what to do or how to escape.

Readers of a seemingly endless barrage of information have an advantage over party goers because they can simply walk away. If you are writing about information, the last thing you want is to lose your reader. Understanding the genres of informational writing is actually helpful to hanging onto your audience.

Genres can have porous borders, as we illustrated in the examples of

The CCSS standard for informational writing: "Write informative/ explanatory texts to examine and convey complex ideas, concepts, and information clearly and accurately through the effective selection, organization, and analysis of content." (CCSSO & NGA, 2010, p. 41)

investigative writing. At the same time, genres have recognizable features. The following excerpt from "Kids Battle the Lure of Junk Food" demonstrates both aspects of informational writing. When students learn to identify these features with the teacher's help, they have a clearer understanding of the expectations of informational writing and also how genres blend.

Mentor Text: "Kids Battle the Lure of Junk Food"

Seattle Times reporter Maureen O'Hagan (2012) provides stories, data, and the testimonies of experts as she investigates the irresistible attraction of junk food.

Nathan Stoltzfus has a problem.

It starts first thing in the morning, when he catches five or 10 minutes of TV just before heading out the door to Northshore Junior High. "There's these commercials for Cookie Crisp cereal or Pop-Tarts," he says. "They show some really happy kids eating them."

Over at school, he makes his way to homeroom as the smell of French toast drifts from the cafeteria.

At lunchtime, he sees a sign over the ice cream and cookies. It says, "Treat yourself today." He tries to focus on his veggie-filled sandwich. But invariably, one of his buddies will jump up for another run through the lunch line. "Who wants to come with me to get some cookies?" the kid'll ask.

To Nathan, this innocent question is a trap. As the heaviest kid at the table, he tells himself, keep your eyes on the veggies. But he also wants to fit in. "It's very tempting," Nathan says. "You feel like you almost have to do it in order to be friends."

Now, Nathan's just 14, but he's no slouch. He's articulate, creative, has a good group of friends and seems to take time to think about what he's doing. He's dedicated, too, singing for years with the Northwest Boychoir.

He's also been overweight for most of his life. To him, it feels like a curse.

And the pressure never subsides. There's the school's annual pie day to celebrate "pi"; there's the group Slurpee runs after school; the torment of his skinny brother devouring Oreos; the weekend trips to the mall. "A couple weeks ago, there was like 16 of us. One of the guys said, 'Oh my gosh you have to try this ice cream,'" he recalls.

What's a kid to do?

Right now, leaders here are trying hard to help. In the past decade, local agencies have been awarded at least $53 million in grants and other funding to combat obesity—most of it in the past year. They've enlisted hundreds of partners in this effort, and they're using some of the most newfangled approaches.

Within the next year, for example, they'll have spent at least $1.8 million getting healthy produce into corner stores. In the next two years, another $276,000 will be spent on building school gardens. Money will go to rejigger

P.E. curriculums, train cafeteria workers and try to get kids to walk to school.

Still, all this effort will miss one of the biggest battlegrounds of all: what's going on inside Nathan's head.

"Treat yourself today," the sign in the cafeteria commands. Just say no, Nathan tries to tell himself. Let's call this the Temptation Complication.

It's a problem for Nathan. It's a problem for tens of thousands of over-weight kids in Washington. And it's a problem for all of us.

It'll take a lot more than school gardens to dig our way out of this one.

People who work on childhood obesity often talk about how different the world was a generation ago. When she was a kid, University of Washington researcher Donna Johnson told me, soda was a special treat. Now, sugar-sweet-ened beverages are just a few quarters away, in the school vending machine. In surveys of Washington adolescents, about 40 percent said they drank at least one soda yesterday.

When he was a kid, former FDA Commissioner David Kessler says, there weren't coffee shops on every corner selling super-duper, fat-and-sugar, grande frappa-yummies. There wasn't the cacophony of chips and cookies at every gas station.

When I was a kid, I recall, we ate pretty much what our parents ate. Now, vast product lines are designed just for youngsters: the Go-Gurts and Lunchables and drink pouches. Experts say more new food products are introduced each year for kids than for adults. And guess what: Studies show kid food has more sugar than the adult version.

And don't even get me started on the "fruit leathers" and "fruit snacks" with nary a drop of juice. "When I was a kid," snickers Margo Wootan, direc-tor of nutrition policy at the Center for Science in the Public Interest, "they were called jelly beans."

This special kid food is sold on special TV stations created just for kids by special advertising execs who study youth culture as if they were researching a doctoral thesis.

Meanwhile, kids are noshing practically nonstop. "Your product doesn't have to be for a meal anymore," says Laurie Demeritt, president of the Bellevue market-research firm the Hartman Group. "Now there are 10 different 'eating occasions' throughout the day."

What we have here is a supply problem. Food is everywhere. That means temptation is everywhere. If Nathan makes healthy choices half the time, it's probably not enough.

But the Temptation Complication has another layer, one that's older than Go-Gurt and Nickelodeon and Mountain Dew. It has to do with biology.

Patsy Treece says her daughter, Hannah, has a "face that radiates kind-ness." She's right. Her eyes are a beautiful brown; her smile shines. At age 13, Treece says, Hannah's the kind of kid who'll stop to help if someone gets hurt on the playground.

She also has an appetite that won't quit.

At dinner, she'll ask for seconds, even thirds. "I'm really, really hungry," she explains.

Well, maybe not hungry exactly.

"It's just that if I see something good," she sighs, "I automatically pick it up and eat it." Like a lot of us, she gets pleasure from food. But afterward, she also feels pain.

Hannah's twin brother is slim and athletic, but her mom is also overweight. Treece has tried different diets with Hannah. She's tried sports. Delay. Portion control, using 100-calorie snack packs. "She'll have a couple of them," Treece says.

Don't even mention Flamin' Hot Cheetos. "She would kill somebody to get a package of those," Treece says. "It's almost like a compulsion." No kidding. Remember the old ad campaign, "Betcha can't eat just one"? That was Lay's Potato Chips. The same company makes Hannah's Cheetos.

Some people simply *can't* stop. There's science to prove it, says former FDA Commissioner Kessler.

Here's a guy who fought Big Tobacco. He's a doctor; he knows what's healthful. Yet until recently, he could come undone over a chocolate-chip cookie. "I have suits in every size," he says ruefully.

Our desire to eat doesn't originate in the stomach, really. We're wired to crave salt, sugar and fat, Kessler says. You see it in laboratory rats, too. They'll brave the possibility of electric shocks to keep eating their junk food. Even *bacteria* swim to sugar.

There's more.

"We used to think people were lazy or it was a question of willpower," Kessler explains. "I can now show you the (brain) scans. The vast majority of people who have a hard time controlling their eating have excessive activation of the brain's emotional core."

When you eat things like cookies or Cheetos you get an immediate reward. You feel good. Your brain actually changes when you eat that stuff, Kessler explains. The neurocircuitry gets rewired. Stumble across a "food cue"—maybe an ad for cereal, or the smell of French toast—and suddenly, your brain lights up. Your thoughts slip into those newly-laid tracks and can't get off, like the way your skis follow along in a cross-country trail. Your brain, Kessler says, gets "hijacked." And the new pathway is reinforced further. Scientists say it's not exactly that we're addicted to food, but it sure is an awful lot like that.

Problem is, these food cues are everywhere. "We're living in a food carnival," Kessler says.

So we're not just fighting temptation like Nathan. We're battling our very biology, that automatic response that makes Kessler crumble at the thought of cookies and Hannah unshakable in the face of orangey-red salt.

Let's call this the Cheeto Compulsion. Betcha can't eat just one.

Hilary Bromberg, strategy director at the Seattle brand/communications firm Egg, says they sometimes put clients through a little exercise: *Talk about your food history.* "They enter almost a trance state," she says. "They say, my grandmother made me this, or my mother made me this. There's this visceral attachment."

Eating, in other words, isn't some sort of clinical calculation of calories. Most people aren't thinking, *Gee, I better have carrots instead of cake because I didn't get my five servings of vegetables today.* "Food is a source of sensual pleasure," Bromberg explains. "The emotions around food are profound." She's saying this as a marketing maven. She's also saying this as someone who studied cognitive neuroscience at Harvard and MIT.

Nathan's mother, Susan Stoltzfus, knows this, too. "Food has been that comfort or that source of consolation or that sense of belonging," she says. It's immediate, too—unlike losing weight, which requires forgoing that sense of pleasure over and over and over. "How do you live for that delayed gratification?" she wonders.

Nathan and Hannah might not explain it the same way. But they understand. Food is pleasure. Food is family, culture and tradition. Food is love.

Let's call this the Comfort Connection. And I'm willing to bet it's within arm's reach right now. (pp. 29–33)

Analyzing and Teaching Features of Informational Writing

Analyzing for the features of informational writing, including purpose and audience, gives students a leg up when it's their turn to write.

Probably the most common way teachers and students talk about a book or an article is in terms of its meaning—an important thing to do, for sure. Another approach is to study a text to discover how it works. What exactly makes it effective? What particular features stand out? Researcher Steve Graham suggests that "teachers and students analyze a text together to identify the most salient features that make it a good text." Graham goes on to say that once students have looked at examples of good, and perhaps also weaker, text, "they can try to create the features in their own writing. Then, with the help of feedback from peers and teachers, they will have an even better understanding of the features" (personal communication, June 13, 2014).

So let's look back at "Kids Battle the Lure of Junk Food" for the elements that make it a good piece of informational writing.

The writing has a *specific purpose*—informing the reader about how and why kids get hooked on junk food. In general, informational writing extends the reader's knowledge about a procedure, a process, or a concept; demonstrates how things work; or explains why things happen.

Such writing has a *focus* and *point of view.* Here is what the author wants you to know about junk food: It's everywhere. It's tempting. It makes you feel good. It's addictive.

The writing has *authority.* The author uses facts and figures, quotes researchers, and amasses evidence and supporting details to establish the significance of the issue. She also coins catchy expressions to mark each of the main points: "Temptation Complication," "Cheeto Compulsion," "Comfort Connection."

In some sense these features seem very clear-cut. But remember the party when an earnest, well-meaning giver of information trapped you? That person had a purpose, focus, point of view, and authority, none of which necessarily engaged you. So what else should the writer share to give the information a little zip, the kind that attracts an audience?

This article about junk food has its own lure. It starts right out with a *story* about a real kid, Nathan, for whom peer pressure just adds to his problems with eating the wrong kinds of food. And then there's Hannah, who is caught in a cycle of pleasure and pain because she eats too much of a good thing. These are likeable, everyday characters, and their stories pull us in and keep us reading.

Although the subject of this article is serious, the *language* doesn't drag us down. Rather, it draws us in and treats us as a community in a conversation. "And don't even get me started on the 'fruit leathers' and 'fruit snacks' with nary a drop of juice," the author tells us. There is no finger wagging here. Rather, the author invites us to share the problem: "It'll take a lot more than school gardens to dig our way out of this one."

An informational article like this one benefits from borrowing or blending other genres. It makes use of *narrative* and *character sketches*. The FDA Commissioner is a doctor who has battled Big Tobacco but can't resist chocolate chip cookies. It establishes a relationship with the reader through informal language while still retaining needed technical terminology like *neurocircuitry*.

The CCSS acknowledge the importance of thoughtfully choosing genre elements *and* of mixing in elements of other genres of writing:

> Students must take task, purpose, and audience into careful consideration, choosing words, information, structures, and formats deliberately. They need to know how to combine elements of different kinds of writing—for example, to use narrative strategies within argument and explanation within narrative—to produce complex and nuanced writing. (CCSO & NGA, 2010, p. 41)

Trying Out Strategies from Reading Models

A savvy teacher might decide to pick out one or two of the salient features of a text and teach students how to manipulate those features. Take the idea of *leads*, for example. It's possible and enjoyable for students to concentrate on that one element, learn more about how it works, and in the process, expand their repertoire of writing strategies.

We noted that "Kids Battle the Lure of Junk Food" grabs the reader's attention with a story:

Nathan Stoltzfus has a problem.

It starts first thing in the morning, when he catches five or 10 minutes of TV just before heading out the door to Northshore Junior High. "There's these commercials for Cookie Crisp cereal or Pop-Tarts, " he says. "They show some really happy kids eating them."

In fact, engaging or highly informative leads are the bread and butter of any good writing. But students may not recognize that they have the license to craft an interesting opening when the writing is not personal or fictional. Even science and history reports can feature openings that dramatize the problem or issue at hand. Good writers think about how to engage their audience.

To start out, teachers and students can compare and contrast different kinds of leads. Together they can select a lead or leads to rewrite. The point of this kind of exercise is to experiment and stretch the boundaries of what a writer can do to attract an audience. The exercise in Figure 3.2 offers students the chance to compare openings and to try their hand at rewriting or inventing alternatives.

Figure 3.2. An Exercise in Inventing New Leads

Read and talk about the opening of *The Grocery Gap: Who Has Access to Healthy Food and Why It Matters*. What does the author do to get your attention? How is this opening different from "Kids Battle the Lure of Junk Food?"

"For millions of Americans—especially people living in low-income communities of color—finding a fresh apple is not so easy. Full-service grocery stores, farmers' markets, and other vendors that sell fresh fruits, vegetables, and other healthy foods cannot be found in their neighborhoods. What can be found, often in great abundance, are convenience stores and fast food restaurants that mainly sell cheap, high-fat, high-sugar, processed foods and offer few healthy options." (Treuhaft & Karpyn, 2010, p. 7)

Your task is to rewrite the opening in four different ways. Use your imagination and keep your reader in mind. Try out each of these strategies with your own sentences:

1. Start with a question: What happens when a community gets too many fast food restaurants?
2. Start with a quotation: "I am sick of running into potholes," my neighbor announced the other day. "This street looks like the face of the moon."
3. Start with a provocative sentence: "Watch out when you enter the park after dark."
4. Start with a close-up and lots of sensory details: "At first glance, the hardware store looks like an abandoned warehouse. The entry sign says 'closed' and the door squeaks in protest when you open it. Once inside, you look in vain for a clerk or some form of life waiting to help you."

Biography: Another Kind of Informational Writing

Informational writing is a big family full of close relatives.

One thing that worries us and many of the teachers we've talked to is that something like informational writing, because the CCSS have spotlighted it, will become fossilized into a single form. What better reason, then, to bring a close relative onto the scene? Biography is a genre within the informational writing family, one that is interesting and accessible enough to show up early in children's writing and still be around in their college writing. Moffett and Wagner (1976) point out that children can write "simple true stories about relatives and friends . . . and later as experienced students, they can write biographies of persons they don't know, basing their true stories on research" (p. 353).

We adapted the following biography assignment from the college end of the spectrum, with the college-ready goal of the CCSS in mind. Professor Stephanie Paterson at California State University–Stanislaus crafted the original so that her 1st-year students could try out the genre for an audience of classmates and practice inquiry and quoting others.

Biography Prompt

Interview a classmate about his or her food loves, food memories, cultural traditions, cooking/baking experiences, notable family recipes, favorite restaurants. Include at least **one direct quotation** (so we can hear the other in his or her own words) and one quality photograph, if you wish.

Thoughts on Lesson Design

Paterson suggests questions for students to use as they interview each other. Students should select several of the following for the initial interview:

- Favorite fast-food place?
- Do you agree with Michael Pollan that "food" needs to be defended?
- What's your favorite junk food? When do you turn to junk food?
- What's your favorite comfort food? When do you crave comfort food?
- Do you make your own choices about your diet or do you have to eat what you're fed?
- What's your favorite food? Why?
- What's your favorite restaurant? Why?
- Do you have any cultural food traditions?

- What types of food do you know how to make?
- Do you have any food allergies?
- How daring are you when it comes to trying new food?
- Do you eat healthy foods?
- What's your least favorite?
- Are you Vegetarian? Vegan? Raw? Omnivore?

Paterson also recommends a second or follow-up interview, selecting the question that received the most interesting answer and asking three focused follow-up questions on the same subject.

Paterson uses the food biographies to help students get acquainted at the beginning of a semester. Students read their pieces to the class as a way of introducing their interview partners. Students might also post their biographies on line or publish them in a print collection.

Conducting interviews and asking follow-up questions are usually accessible activities for both middle and high school students, and are certainly socially enjoyable. The most difficult part of this kind of informational assignment is writing up the interview in some kind of engaging, coherent manner. Both parts of the process will most likely require modeling and rehearsal.

DIVING DEEPER:
FROM INFORMATION TO ARGUMENT

Consider the following multiple-choice question:

The worst thing that can happen when I teach students to write arguments is:
   a. Their papers will be full of opinions but alarmingly short of evidence.
   b. They will flounder all over the place so I will have to resort to the five-paragraph essay.
   c. Their words will be stiff and boring, unlike the words in their personal narratives.
   d. The students themselves will be stiff and boring.
   e. I will be stiff and boring.
   f. All of the above.

> The CCSS standard for argumentative writing: "Write arguments to support claims in an analysis of substantive topics or texts, using valid reasoning and relevant and sufficient evidence" (CCSSO & NGA, 2010, p. 41).

Although it is technically impossible for "f" to be correct because the respondent is asked to choose "the worst," if you chose "f," you are probably in the majority. That's because you know the big challenges when it comes to teaching argument: how to work with students in making and supporting claims, organizing their arguments, and doing so without sacrificing voice and style.

The following case study illustrates how teachers can frame lessons that draw on local knowledge, personal experience, and recognizable features of a particular genre.

Case Study: Writing Restaurant Reviews

California State University–Stanislaus Professor Stephanie Paterson invites her composition students to eat out and write about what they discover:

> A good food review is often part description, part narration (storytelling), and part argumentation.
>
> You pick the place. There are a number of restaurants within walking distance of the campus (e.g., *Vito's, Sushi Garden II, The Taco Shop, Pantogh's*). Or you might choose a landmark restaurant in Turlock, like *Latiff's Diner* or another establishment in the older part of town. Or you might compare and contrast one or two nearby taco trucks. Or you might select Mom's on campus.
>
> You determine the audience for this writing (college kids on a shoestring budget, food adventurers, or faculty new to the Turlock–Modesto area). The target audience(s) you select will shape how you go about writing this piece.

And so the journey begins. At the start line, students study online restaurant reviews and bring a restaurant review to class. From there, they look at the commonalties among reviews. What are the elements? Some are numerical: star ratings and costs. The more complex elements deal with the quality of the food and service, the atmosphere or decor, the overall experience, and the specifics: menu items that please or displease.

Then comes the real fun. Students visit a local restaurant. "They take notes while they eat," Paterson explains. "They talk to restaurant owners and patrons. Some of them go with classmates or boyfriends or family. These people are eventually written into their reviews. The important thing is the students' role as ethnographers. It shifts their perceptions and helps them observe more fully, like reading walls or looking at other customers" (personal communication, June 12, 2014). In the final analysis, readers expect a certain content and pattern in a restaurant review. Paterson notes, "I make a big deal about genres, the fact that they're social and there are conventions to each one of them. I also make a big deal of factual observations, learning to pay attention, to make something out of what you see, to take notes. These are huge tools in a writer's arsenal."

The rubric in Figure 3.3 represents a collaborative effort, constructed after students have combed through sample published restaurant reviews and identified the stand-out traits. According to Paterson, the rubric "emerges mid-process and then at the end as the assessment tool." Recognizing that rubrics are potentially limiting, Paterson makes a point of highlighting

Figure 3.3. A Rubric for Restaurant Reviews

1. The piece has a distinctive *voice* and *point of view*. The writer situates him/herself in the story, and describes his or /her relationship to the place, and establishes his/her *purpose* for choosing this food establishment.

   1   2   3   4   5

2. The piece has *a catchy lead* (or) opening paragraph that makes the reader want to read on.

   1   2   3   4   5

3. In the body of the food review, the writer approaches the subject from *several different perspectives* (i.e., the writer offers details of the restaurant, the overall atmosphere, descriptions of what he/she ordered; the writer provides a sense of the menu, describes the service, ambiance and decor, describes his/her favorite menu item, describes the food and presentation, answers the question of whether or not this place is "vegetarian friendly," and provides readers with pricing information).

   1   2   3   4   5

4. The writer provides a *thoughtful and clear* conclusion in which he or she offers a summary of the overall dining experience.

   1   2   3   4   5

5. The writing has been *carefully edited* line by line to correct spelling and punctuation errors, to make sure there are consistent verb tenses, no confusing shifts in the point of view, and all proper names have been capitalized.

   1   2   3   4   5

6. *Issues of style:* This writing replicates the genre of restaurant reviews. Place names are in italics (e.g., *Latiff's Diner*), a minimum of one quality photograph has been included, the title for this food review is in BOLD, with the writer's name underneath it in italics. The piece ends with an "Overall Product Rating: 1–5 stars).

   1   2   3   4   5

"something done well that doesn't exist on the rubric or goes beyond the rubric."

Student Writing. Here is a paper from Paterson's class. Note that this student's writing demonstrates her understanding of the restaurant review genre, especially in her attention to audience.

Mexican Food Without Spiciness

By Miriam Espinosa

Shopping can be a little exhausting and more so if you have not had anything to eat in hours. Merced Mall has a good variety of restaurants that offer all kinds of food. I did not know what to eat; all I knew was that my stomach was growling. Panda Express seemed too usual, since all of my mall visits end there. I wanted to try a different kind of food and Mexican food seemed to be a good option.

Maria's Taco Shop is a little restaurant located next to Panda Express. The kitchen seemed to be very spacious. The walls had white and shiny tile, which gave the look of a traditional Mexican kitchen. On the front wall, there were pictures of the menu and a brief description of the ingredients. Right next to the pictures is the salsa bar with different kinds of salsas, lemons, radishes, chilies and carrots that you can add to your food for extra taste.

Maria's Taco Shop has a gigantic yellow sign with the extensive menu on it, which makes it difficult to avoid. The menu offers many choices, including combination plates, side dishes, and entrées. Everything on the menu seems so mouth watering that you are going to have a hard time deciding what to order. After a thoughtful decision I decided to place my order. The friendly gentleman that took my order was willing to explain what each dish contained. I ordered a torta de chorizo ($4.99), flautas ($3.99) and a medium agua de horchata ($1.80).

My order arrived approximately ten minutes later. The flautas which are rolled tacos had meat inside, some had ground beef and others had chicken. The flautas were fried which made them really crispy and at the end made you thirsty. Luckily, they were spread over the top with fresh lettuce, tomato, guacamole and yellow cheese which added a unique flavor. The torta de chorizo which is very similar to a sandwich, as its name indicates had chorizo, as well as beans, lettuce, tomato, guacamole and yellow cheese. I found a piece of plastic on the torta which I know came from the chorizo. The chorizo is usually in a long plastic bag and you have to cut it, in order to take the chorizo out and cook it. The chef was in a hurry and did not notice that a piece of plastic was in the food. Both, the torta and flautas were not spicy. Mexican food is not complete without the spiciness of the chile, which is why I had to stop by the salsa bar and add some salsa for extra spiciness. Just in case I got hot, I made sure that my agua de horchata, a drink made out of rice, was handy. The drink was a little too sweet for my taste but still refreshing. The total was $10.78.

Other items on the menu include the Child's Special ($3.00), Camarones a La Diabla ($9.99), Menudo ($5.50) and Vegetarian Burritos ($4.25). The menu ranges from $1.75 to $9.99, which are reasonable prices for tasty food. They have a variety of non-alcoholic beverages, usually sodas and tropical drinks (horchata, jamaica and tamarindo) which come in two sizes 16 oz and 32 oz.

The atmosphere is very calm; you can have an intimate conversation without the necessity of screaming. There is a place with tables and chairs where all the people from the different restaurants sit to enjoy their delicious food. Usually during lunch time it is hard to find a table. The dress code seemed to be very casual.

I had a good experience at Maria's Taco Shop. I will definitely return for all my craving for Mexican food when I cannot get them at home. Maria's Taco Shop has a variety of meals that anybody can afford. The food is in a good quality and in a big quantity. The service is exceptional and employees are always glad to help. I will definitely recommend Maria's Taco Shop to anyone that wishes to eat fast, tasty and low-priced Mexican food.

Restaurant Information: *Maria's Taco Shop*
Rating: *** (good)
Price: $ ($1.75–$9.99)
Service: Friendly, willing to explain what each of the dishes contains.
Ambience: Calm, lots of people eating from the adjacent restaurants.
Location: 701 Merced Mall, Merced CA; (209) 388-9303
Hours: Mon.-Sat. Open 9am-9pm, Sun. 9am-6pm
Payment Information: Cash and all major credit cards

A Big Question in Teaching Writing: The Elephant in the Room

For those who read reviews, Espinosa's writing reads like a classic. It seems that hardly anyone can make a decision these days without reading what someone else has to say about a product or movie or book or restaurant. But would anyone read a review that begins "I like Maria's Taco Shop. There are three reasons why I like this restaurant." So why is the five-paragraph essay so widespread in the teaching of opinion writing?

The choice to teach form before content is deeply rooted in classroom practice because form is tangible, clear-cut, and seemingly gives students a handy structure when it comes time to take tests. Yet, often that choice can backfire.

From the student's point of view, the five-paragraph essay format is a welcome prop, until the time comes when it's not enough. Melanie Sperling recalls a teary student who came to her office at the University of California–Berkeley, paper in hand, to find out why he received a "C." "I just don't understand what you want," he said, "I had my 'what' and 'three whys'" (personal communication, June 12, 2014).

Another Berkeley student wrote an essay about having to unlearn this well-learned formula.

> "Do not write a five paragraph essay. Not all paragraphs have to be the same size. Topic sentences don't always have to be at the beginning of each paragraph." These words from my professor, Gail Offen-Brown, completely shocked me on my first day of College Writing R1A. Her words contradicted everything I learned in high school: every essay required the traditional five paragraphs with six to eight sentences in each paragraph. Topic sentences needed to be at the beginning of the paragraphs—all of which were now thrown out the window. I struggled to adjust to this new form of unconventional writing. (Trinh Nguyen, quoted in Smith, 2005, p. 1)

Students' struggles to shed the formula—to deprogram themselves from adhering to a given structure—worries writing experts like Laura Stokes. When she taught writing and directed the composition program at the University of California–Davis, Stokes (1990) observed that too often students who relied on the five-paragraph format were unable to engage in the intellectual work of writing because they:

- Imposed a structure on the task instead of attending to what the assignment really asked of them
- Wrote essays in which the body paragraphs failed to relate to each other in any "fully articulated, or even discernable way" (p. 2)
- Wrote essays that contained "collections of randomly ordered, equally weighted parts of a topic," instead of essays with hierarchically ordered ideas (p. 6)

In sum, Stokes viewed the five-paragraph formula as an inhibitor of "critical, conceptual, creative thinking" (p. 6).

Arguably, the five-paragraph scheme has inspired more discussion than any other notion about structure. One middle school teacher, Ray Skjelbred, (2005) even wrote a poem about it:

The Five-Paragraph Essay
They thought abstract thinking had become too messy,
So they invented the five-paragraph essay.
Which gave the illusion of order and symmetry

But pushed each voice into anonymity.
Such formulaic steps could be charted on a graph,
that could serve as a writing process epitaph.
Sentences of particularity are the heart of writing.
That's why this form is worth fighting.
It's a strange frame, where words turn to dregs
In a crude little nest without any eggs.

Our point here is not to denigrate structure, or to remove the teaching of structure from the curriculum, but rather to think in terms of multiple structures as opposed to a single one. And in the pecking order of what comes first—content or structure—let content be the front-runner and the determiner of structure.

As a first step in helping students with structure, Paterson identifies some characteristics of the restaurant review genre: "A good food review is often part *description,* part *narration (storytelling)* and part *argumentation"* (personal communication, April 13, 2013). The second step is to give students a more specific idea of what the content should be and in what order. Paterson uses the rubric to accomplish this by describing the opening, body, and conclusion. In particular, the information Paterson gives her students about the body gives them a roadmap for both content and organization:

> The writer offers details of the restaurant, the overall atmosphere, descriptions of what he/she ordered. The writer provides a sense of the menu, describes the service, ambiance and décor, describes his/her favorite menu item, describes the food and presentation, answers the question of whether or not this place is "vegetarian friendly," and provides readers with pricing information. (personal communication, April 13, 2013)

There are many ways to highlight content and organization for students. We endorse Paterson's collaborative approach to developing a rubric. With or without a rubric, teachers and students can work from models to identify elements of the genre and the way they play out in content and organization.

Developing Content for an Argument

The CCSS emphasize having students "conduct short as well as more sustained research" in order to "build and present knowledge" (p. 41).

Had Paterson limited her students to five paragraphs, she would have drastically limited the content of their reviews. But once students break out of the cage and are free to roam, they need a different kind of support: how to find enough content to say something significant and substantive.

Hillocks's inquiry approach, which we mentioned earlier, is all about building content. In fact, Hillocks (2011) recommends that students be allowed to muck around, gathering and analyzing information on the many sides of an issue before adopting a position and making a claim:

> Although many teachers begin to teach some version of argument with the writing of a thesis statement, in reality, good argument begins with looking at the data that are likely to become the evidence in an argument and that give rise to a thesis statement or major claim. . . . without analysis of any data (verbal and nonverbal texts, materials, surveys and samples), any thesis is likely to be no more than a preconception or assumption or clichéd popular belief that is unwarranted and, at worst, totally indefensible. For that reason, my students and I have approached the teaching of argument from the examination of data as a first step. (pp. xxi–xxii)

Notably, the CCSS allude to the importance of content by placing the standards on research in the writing section—exactly where research should be if students are to build material for their writing. The classic method of accumulating enough information to make an argument is to read, read, read, and then read some more. One of the reasons the CCSS emphasize basing writing on reading is to help students build content. No one would argue against reading widely to prepare an argument, and everyone seems to know how to whip out an iPad or cellphone and instantly Google for information or evidence. What are additional ways of building content?

Ask Someone. Community college teacher Laury Fischer helps his students discover multiple resources and word-of-mouth recommendations. Before any writing occurs, each student writes down his or her chosen topic on a piece of paper. The papers then circulate throughout the class where other students make suggestions about what to read, who to talk to, where to visit, and so on. Fischer emphasizes the need for interview contacts because "that's where people are usually shy and need an 'oh, my uncle is a social worker—you can talk to him' kind of thing" (personal communication, June 12, 2014). He also encourages students to use emails, texts, and Twitter so they can communicate outside of class to let each other know when they come across something on TV or someone interesting to interview. In other words, Fischer has his students do what any one of us would do when faced with a question or a project: Ask someone who might be able to give us some tips. Exchange information. Keep each other posted.

Take a Survey. Firsthand research is often more exciting for students than reading about research conducted by others. For example, if students wanted to argue that fast food plays an important role in an individual's or family's life, they might collect evidence for this claim through a survey that explores reasons for relying on fast food. Conversely, students might find a survey beneficial to help support a claim that healthy food is becoming more prevalent in local households. While there are many ways to help students conduct a survey, we will suggest two of them here:

1. Take students through the process of framing several questions for their survey, using guidelines such as the following:
   - Clearly state why you are taking the survey.
   - Include instructions with your survey questionnaire.
   - Keep questions short, concise, and unbiased.
   - Ask only one question at a time.
   - Use the appropriate type of question:
     » Structured questions that offer the respondent a set of answers from which to choose (a, b, c)
     » Rating questions that capture attitude or opinion (unsatisfied to extremely satisfied)
     » Open-ended questions that ask for more than a one-word answer (why? how?)
   - Order and or group questions according to subject.
   - Test the survey questionnaire.
2. If technology is an option, take students directly to an online tool like SurveyMonkey (www.surveymonkey.com).

Begin with Local Knowledge, Personal Experience, and Recognizable Criteria. Another way to build content for tasks like restaurant reviews or other kinds of evaluative writing is to develop standards for the writer's opinion.

> Students need practice in generating criteria, in stating a claim (in the case of evaluation, a claim of judgment), and in building their arguments. Practice in these areas carries over into all of the argumentative writing types.
>
> Criteria are standards for judging something. They apply to a class of things, not to individuals in the class. If, for example, students are to evaluate a fast-food restaurant, their criteria must be appropriate for fast-food restaurants, not for gourmet restaurants. For evaluations to seem informed and convincing, they must be based on appropriate criteria. (California Department of Education, 1993, p. 68)

Teacher and writer Art Peterson (1996) recommends that students practice developing criteria for judging some of the following items. "At their best," he asks, "what qualities do they have?"

- a hamburger
- a rock group
- ice cream

- a supermarket
- a musical video
- a dentist
- a soap opera
- a teacher
- an automobile
- a fast-food restaurant
- a perfect weekend
- a politician (p. 56)

Combine First- and Secondhand Research. As illustrated by the next case study, students build content by using several different resources and strategies:

- Engaging in print reading *and* in "reading" an event or place or situation: One is secondhand research and one is firsthand.
- Spending significant time accumulating material for their writing.
- Pulling together their own experiences, their observations, and their readings on the way to making an argument.
- Collaborating in all phases of the reading, research, and writing.

Case Study: "Reading" the Farmers' Market

"Where does your family buy food?" Gail Offen-Brown, a lecturer at UC Berkeley, sends her 1st-year composition students out to farmers' markets with this question, among others, in mind. "I encourage you to go with other students in the class," she says. "Take a notebook and pen to write down observations and interviews" (all Offen-Brown quotes in this section are from a personal communication, May 15, 2013).

It's not surprising that her students love the idea of getting out of the classroom and of assuming the role of ethnographers. Rarely do students consider where food comes from, notes Offen-Brown. "And some of these kids have never heard of a farmers' market while others, particularly kids from other countries, consider them old and traditional." Their reactions? "They are very taken by the free samples," says Offen-Brown. "And by how nice everyone is. People have conversations and social interactions that are not part of shopping in a supermarket. The whole scene—the carnival at-mosphere—appeals to students. Of course, they comment on how good the food tastes and on products they have never seen anywhere else."

But Offen-Brown's students are not preparing to write an argument for or against farmers' markets. Their questions and observations are more nu-anced and complex. Who goes to farmers' markets? How do they get there? Do you need a car? A big wallet? To what extent do farmers' markets offer a new social and economic space, as Michael Pollan (2010) proposes in his article "Food Fight."

Students take copious field notes as they consider these questions. Offen-Brown instructs them to write down what they see, hear, smell, touch, and taste. "You may also want to interview shoppers and sellers. In an interview, be sure to introduce yourself as a Cal student and your project."

So where does this investigation of farmers' markets lead? Straight to a piece of argumentative writing in which students have to pull together (synthesize) a lot of material: their field notes, their own experiences as shoppers, and the ideas of Michael Pollan who writes that farmers' markets create a space removed from the influence of big corporations and government. This is their assignment:

> For this essay, you are to visit and closely observe (as Pollan puts it, hang around) a local farmer's market. To what extent do your observations bear out Pollan's view of farmers' markets? To what extent does the specific market that you visit constitute "a new social and economic space" and in what particular ways? What, if any, limitations do you see in Pollan's analysis? In other words, this essay asks you to use Pollan's ideas as a frame for examining the farmers' market and making your own argument.

According to Offen-Brown, students can easily write descriptions of a farmers' market and, yes, their opinions. But turning these into an academic essay is another matter. Offen-Brown invites students to share "what you're thinking about arguing" so they can look together at "what evidence supports what ideas." In the end, they have to write paragraphs driven by claims rather than by a chronology of experiences—a challenging rhetorical move even for the best of writers.

Another Look at Argument: Where Should We Buy Our Food?

We have modeled the following assignment on Offen-Brown's. The reading is difficult, but not as challenging as the college-level reading, and the writing assignment has fewer layers. Like the restaurant review and farmer's market assignments, this one combines reading, first- and secondhand research, and collaboration.

With the CCSS in mind, notice that this assignment:

- Integrates reading, writing, speaking, listening
- Requires research based on focused questions
- Requires close reading to determine what the text says
- Reinforces the need for evidence in support of arguments

- Asks writers to combine elements of different kinds of writing
- Invites students to work collaboratively to build on others' ideas

Reading Assignment. In his book, *In Defense of Food*, Michael Pollan (2008) gives his own set of rules for eating well. One of them is to hang around farmers' markets instead of supermarkets.

GET OUT OF THE SUPERMARKET WHENEVER POSSIBLE. You won't find any high-fructose corn syrup at the farmers' market. You also won't find any elaborately processed food products, any packages with long lists of unpronounceable ingredients or dubious health claims, nothing microwavable, and, perhaps best of all, no old food from far away. What you will find are fresh whole foods picked at the peak of their taste and nutritional quality—precisely the kind your great grandmother, or even your Neolithic ancestors, would easily have recognized as food.

Indeed, the surest way to escape the Western diet is simply to depart the realms it rules: the supermarket, the convenience store, and the fast-food outlet. It is hard to eat badly from the farmers' market, from a CSA box (community-supported agriculture, an increasingly popular scheme in which you subscribe to a farm and receive a weekly box of produce), or from your garden. The number of farmers' markets has more than doubled in the last ten years, to more than four thousand, making it one of the fastest-growing segments of the food marketplace. It is true that most farmers' markets operate only seasonally, and you won't find everything you need there. But buying as much as you can from the farmers' market, or directly from the farm when that's an option, is a simple act with a host of profound consequences for your health as well as for the health of the food chain you've now joined.

When you eat from the farmers' market, you automatically eat food that is in season, which is usually when it is most nutritious. Eating in season also tends to diversify your diet—because you can't buy strawberries or broccoli or potatoes twelve months of the year, you'll find yourself experimenting with other foods when they come into the market. . . . Cooking is one of the most important health consequences of buying food from local farmers; for one thing, when you cook at home you seldom find yourself reaching for the ethoxylated diglycerides or high-fructose corn syrup. But more on cooking later.

To shop at a farmers' market or sign up with a CSA is to join a short food chain that has several implications for your health. Local produce is typically picked ripe and is fresher than supermarket produce, and for those reasons it should be tastier and more nutritious. As for supermarket organic produce, it too is likely to have come from far away—from the industrial organic farms of California or, increasingly, China. And while it's true that the organic label guarantees that no synthetic pesticides or fertilizers have been used to produce the food, many, if not most, of the small farms that supply farmers' markets are organic in everything but name. . . .

If you're concerned about chemicals in your produce, you can simply ask the farmer at the market how he or she deals with pests and fertility and begin the sort of conversation between producers and consumers that, in the end, is the best guarantee of quality in your food. So many of the problems of the industrial food chain stem from its length and complexity. A wall of ignorance intervenes between consumers and producers, and that wall fosters a certain carelessness on both sides. Farmers can lose sight of the fact that they're growing food for actual eaters rather than for middlemen, and consumers can easily forget that growing good food takes care and hard work. In a long food chain, the story and identity of the food (Who grew it? Where and how was it grown?) disappear into the undifferentiated stream of commodities, so that the only information communicated between consumers and producers is a price. In a short food chain, eaters can make their needs and desires known to the farmer, and farmers can impress on eaters the distinctions between ordinary and exceptional food, and the many reasons why exceptional food is worth what it costs. Food reclaims its story, and some of its nobility, when the person who grew it hands it to you. So here's a subclause to the get-out-of-the-supermarket rule: *Shake the hand that feeds you.* (pp. 157–160)

Argumentative Writing Prompt

Michael Pollan claims that farmers' markets have a number of benefits that are not found in supermarkets or quick-stop shops. He argues that shoppers should actually avoid supermarkets whenever possible in order to find fresh food that is locally grown and free of chemicals. What do you think?

Write an argument in favor of farmers' markets, supermarkets, or any other place you advocate for buying food. Remember to provide evidence and to explain how the evidence supports your claim.

Thoughts on Lesson Design

Success with this assignment, like all others, depends on students coming up with a substantial amount of content. Here are a few suggestions for helping them along:

1. Invite students to visit one or more places for buying food and provide them with focused questions for their inquiry, such as:
   » Who are the other shoppers?
   » How do you get to the market? Do you need a car?
   » When is the market open?
   » What kind of food does it sell?
   » What are the prices?
   » What benefits do you see in shopping in this market?
   » What are the disadvantages?

2. Give students time to read and research.
3. Ask students to interview family members or friends who do the shopping. Where do they shop and why?
4. Make a class pros and cons list (e.g., farmers' markets feature fresh, in-season produce but a limited selection of food overall; supermarkets offer 24/7 access to groceries, including online ordering, but do not guarantee that food is local or fresh).

In the next chapter, we will discuss more ideas for scaffolding and spiraling writing assignments and processes. But note that our sequence of assignments is in itself a form of scaffolding or spiraling. Students practice narrative, investigative writing, informational writing, and evaluation (review) on their way to argument. This means they may have learned enough to pop an anecdote or a chunk of information into their arguments. (You can remind them!)

Writing for All Seasons: Teaching Argument in the Content Areas

One of the mantras that emerged from the first summer institute of the Bay Area Writing Project, inspired by UC University Professor Emerita of English Josephine Miles, went something like this: *A person never learns to write once and for all.* This adage certainly qualifies as a good news/bad news message for teachers of writing, whose job, it seems, will never be done, as well as for writers themselves.

The truth is that over their lifetime, writers encounter new situations and disciplines with unfamiliar requirements for writing. And while it's not possible to prepare for every twist and turn, students who write regularly in math, science, history, social studies, and even auto shop have more tools at their disposal when they run headlong into the unexpected.

The idea of range, or versatility, then, extends to writing in the content areas for the purposes of learning the content itself and also learning the rhetorical features of the discipline. No single teacher is going to teach the gamut, of course. But teachers, particularly those who collaborate, have tackled the notion of range realistically and successfully. The trick is to involve all or most of the teachers in a school.

Because Writing Matters, a book written by the National Writing Project and Carl Nagin (2003), offers this suggestion: "In many schools, English teachers have the main responsibility for teaching writing. But districts and schools that have made writing an overarching curricular aim have done so by declaring it the job of all faculty and by providing ongoing professional development focused on writing. A key element in such systemic change is finding a core group of teachers who write and are enthusiastic about teaching it" (p. 17).

Case Study: Content Area Teachers Join Forces to Teach Argument

Corine Maday and Marleigh Williams teach a class called Foods and Nutrition at a rural high school in Northern California. Their 11th- and 12th-grade students tend to live on fast food and shy away from anything that is "too green." According to Williams, "they quibble when they have to put broccoli in a broccoli casserole." But Maday says kids are also curious about healthy choices. The question is how to engage these students in the politics and economics of the food they eat, as well as in everyday considerations like serving sizes, calories, additives, and preservatives.

Maday and Williams have a special edge. They participated in the Northern California Writing Project's Content Area Literacy Network where they collaborated with other rural high school teachers on reading and writing strategies that support student learning in content areas.[1] The result was a curriculum unit called Fast Food vs. Slow Food.

For starters, the two teachers provided readings so that students—randomly divided into advocates for "fast" food and advocates for "slow" food—had the information they needed for a class debate pitting the ease, reliability, and affordability of fast food against the health and communal benefits of slow food. To scaffold the readings, the teachers provided graphic organizers—reshaped from typical squares and circles into bunches of carrots and packets of French fries.

Their reading and mapping introduced students to our modern food expressway with its confusing, often obfuscating road signs. From there, they jumped into discussions, quick writes, and even taste tests that compared Chips Ahoy chocolate chip cookies with their rival homemade version. In the end, they were able to pick a "side" and argue for it.

These teachers did what content area teachers do best: They armed their students with content information and folded in essential literacy activities to help them unpack, summarize, and analyze the information. Did the students have the necessary background to argue for a way of eating? Yes. Did most of them argue for slow food? Yes. Did they stop patronizing fast-food restaurants? No. But as Maday and Williams told them, you will come back to these lessons at another time in your life, and they will serve you well. True. And lessons like these—with their practical, relevant, sequenced interplay of reading, writing, speaking, and listening—will also serve students well as they encounter their next academic or workplace assignments.

---

1. The Content Area Literacy Network: A Rural Counties Collaborative is a partnership of Corning Union High School District, the Northern California Writing Project, the Chico State Education Department, the Tehama County Office of Education, Yreka High School, Modoc High School, Hamilton City High School, and Butte College. It is supported by the California Post-Secondary Education Commission's Improving Teacher Quality grant program.

Student Writing. One advantage of writing arguments in subjects like science is the amount of readily available content. When students write about that content, they not only learn it, they also make use of it.

Slow Food

By Monica DeCasper

My opinion on slow food is it looks better, tastes better, smells better, and of course it is healthier for you than fast food. Slow food has less fat than fast food and you can save more than 150 calories and save $6 dollars a day. My argument in support of slow food over fast food is that the health benefits largely outweigh the benefits of fast food.

When you eat slow food you have the opportunity of choosing healthier food options that afford you a well-balanced diet whereas fast food can leave you fighting with consequences later on and regrettably lead to obesity especially in children. Choosing to eat slow food is more beneficial than choosing greasy fast food. With choosing slow food, you know where and when you bought it and how long it has been in your refrigerator unlike choosing to eat fast food when you don't know how long the food has been sitting there. Unlike fast food, slow food is fresh and it is good for you to eat.

More people these days go out to eat instead of eating at there own house but if your trying to loose weight or eat healthier fast food is the quickest way to ruin your efforts. With choosing slow food you can choose a cup of fresh organic vegetables over a carton of greasy over-priced fries. You can choose a grilled chicken Caesar salad with light vinaigrette dressing over an over-processed fatty hamburger. Your metabolism and heart works harder to break down greasy fast food. Eating healthy doesn't mean you have to give up fast food all together, it just means eat fast food in moderation.

Slow food affords you the ability to save money, watch calorie and sodium intake and to choose healthier options over the easy drive-thru option. Fast food will take its toll not only on your body but also on your wallet in the long run if your not careful. With eating slow food you are saving your body, your wallet and numerous visits to the doctor.

Thoughts on Content Area Writing

This writer incorporates specific facts and examples as she compares the relative merits of slow food over fast food. She avoids simply listing or reciting what she knows, or falling into a more simplistic, less nuanced argument for one side only. Rather, she takes up the pros and cons, makes applications to real-world problems like losing weight, and gives practical suggestions for the kinds of food that are healthy. While the piece is not error free, her control over the content is strong.

Expanding the Possibilities for Writing

At a recent Writing Project institute at UC Berkeley, teacher–participants cracked open the big-three writing categories as they appear in the CCSS. In fairness, the CCSS do not present a do-this-and-only-this approach to types of writing. However, it would be easy to miss the fact that these broad categories—narrative, informational, and argumentative—are umbrellas for a whole host of genres. Why limit ourselves?

In that spirit, the teachers put together an extended list of possibilities under each of the three CCSS types. Notice in Figure 3.4 on the next page that some genres, like nominations, campaign speeches, apologies, and complaints, appear more than once and under different headings. It's those porous borders at work. When it comes to writing, the range should not be fenced off. New genres crop up overnight. Suddenly, we have blogs and tweets. Who knows what's next?

LAST THOUGHTS

First—Have Fun

Read, inquire, and write about things that interest you and your students. You don't have to stick with food as a topic You don't have to stick with one pathway for informational or any other kind of writing. Go on the road less taken. As Figure 3.4 indicates, a biography is informational. So is a travel piece. So are the ins and outs of baseball and other games. Teacher and author Kelly Gallagher (2011) reminds us, "The day our students lose touch with the joy of inquiry and their sense of intellectual curiosity is the day I want to stop teaching" (p. 134).

Second—Take Time

So many things to teach, so little time. So many books to read, so many papers to write, so many questions to answer, so many lives to touch. There isn't a teacher alive who doesn't struggle with how to slice up time, which always seems to be on backorder. The activities and assignments that develop students' versatility—activities such as reading, talking, listening, investigating, inquiring, analyzing, and practicing—are sure to gobble up more time than ever. There are few shortcuts when it comes to intellectual work.

Figure 3.4. Possibilities for Writing

Informational	Argumentative	Narrative
Scientific report	Advertisements	Personal narratives
Historical report	Editorials	Ballads
Research paper	Letters to editors	Poetry
Biographies	Book reviews	Fables
Autobiographies	Movie reviews	Stories
Historical recounts	Restaurant reviews	Anecdotes
Travel writing	Food reviews	Personal recounts
Directions	Evaluations	Vignettes
Instructions	Complaints	Songs
Agendas	Apologies	Fairy tales
Recipes	Nominations	Myths
Manuals	Proposals	Legends
Rules for games	Campaign speeches	Haiku
Scientific explanations	Advice columns	Speeches
Technical explanations		Jokes
Life explanations		Personal essays
Complaints		Social commentary
Apologies		Novels
Invitations		Memoirs
Introductions		Plays
Nominations		
Proposals		
Campaign speeches		
Interviews		
Survey results		
Advice columns		

CHAPTER 4

Spiraling and Scaffolding

The concept of *spiraling* seems somewhat serpentine, and well, circuitous. In fact, the circular approach—revisiting concepts over months and across grades—strengthens learning and moves students to more sophisticated understandings. It's not a new idea, nor an invention by the writers of the Common Core State Standards. John Dewey came up with a spiral as a metaphor for learning way back in 1938. In the 1960s, Jerome Bruner became the champion of a spiral curriculum, getting a 5-decade jump on the CCSS. Bruner (1960) described it as a design in which key concepts are presented repeatedly throughout the grade levels, but with deepening layers of complexity or in different applications each time. According to Bruner, we should not hold off introducing youngsters to new ideas or skills. In fact, just the opposite. We should take every opportunity to open up the world as early as possible with the caveat that we take into account a child's age and experience.

CAPTURING THE BIG IDEA OF SPIRALING

One good way to understand spiraling is to imagine life without it. Three- and four-year-olds, as we know, are not really ready to play soccer. Their toes refuse to locate the ball dead-on, and when they run, it's often in circles. So do their parents explain that they must wait until they are 10 or 11 to mess around on the soccer field? What about young artists? Do we snatch a crayon from a preschooler and say, "Please hold off until you're 12 when you are more likely to draw a proper mountain or tree"?

The truth is that most parents and grandparents can hardly wait to get a child up and running. What's more, Bruner says the important thing is to start where kids are. Take the sport of basketball. No very young child has the height, coordination, or even hand size to dribble and shoot the way James Naismith, the 1891 inventor of basketball, envisioned. For that reason, most kids' leagues use a smaller ball, lower basket, and shorter foul line. Many leagues modify the rules so that youngsters can bounce the ball once or twice, then catch it and run, with referees being very lenient on the interpretation of traveling. In other words, children do not have to wait until all their growth hormones kick in to play basketball.

It's almost embarrassing to realize that prescribed curricula sometimes hold children back. Bruner (1960), for one, thought so: "Schools may be wasting precious years by postponing the teaching of many important subjects on the grounds that they are too difficult." Rather, Bruner says, "Any subject can be taught effectively in some intellectually honest form to any child at any stage of development" (p. 33).

Now consider the idea of grade-by-grade standards in the CCSS. Are they meant to put the brakes on when teachers can introduce new concepts to students? For example, the idea of *counterarguments* (acknowledging alternate or opposing claims) pops up for the first time in grade 7. Does this signal that teachers should wait until students are 12 or 13 to deal with the fact that people have different opinions on different issues?

The answer, of course, is no. The CCSS ELA writers had a clear intention when they developed the grade-level standards, namely, that students not go beyond a certain grade level *without* understanding a particular concept or accomplishing a certain skill, for example, addressing counterarguments. In other words, the grade-level progressions mark where students should be by a certain point in time, *not* when things should first be taught. However, a common misinterpretation is that the progressions are a step-by-step guide for curriculum—as if we should all hold our collective breaths and wait until a certain moment to spring a new idea on students.

Arthur Applebee (2013), one critic of the CCSS grade-level progressions, recognizes the danger in "focusing curriculum and instruction directly on the standards themselves" because doing so may create an emphasis for curriculum and instruction that is not anchored in the way reading, writing, and language skills actually develop—through applying "available skills to ever more complex and specialized texts and tasks" (p. 28).

> The grade-level progressions are not a beginning, nor are they a finish line. Learning is ongoing.

In effect, Applebee is making a case for spiraling. And that's where this chapter begins—with concrete classroom examples of spiraling. The second half of the chapter focuses on scaffolding: things like modeling, mapping, and tapping into prior knowledge. Scaffolding gives students the support they need to jump ahead; it builds the bridge between what they know and what they will learn; it's the basketball hoop, lowered slightly, so the young player can shoot the ball in the air and through the net. The idea of tying scaffolding to spiraling may not be new, but in terms of writing, the combination is central to getting better.

TAKING THE PLUNGE:
EXPLORING SPIRALING TECHNIQUES

Spiraling occurs when a previous lesson or learning takes on new dimensions.

That early "show, don't tell" lesson—one that may have first cropped up in grade school—can be the genesis of subsequent lessons for years to come. In Chapter 2, we explored various ways that secondary teachers add depth and sophistication to students' initial encounters with "showing" strategies. It's also possible and desirable to move the concepts of "showing" and "telling" to an entirely different kind of writing—a classic example of what Bruner meant by repeating a concept, but in a different application.

In the following excerpt from a college placement exam, a high school student makes a case for the importance of preserving memories. The prompt asks writers to take a position on whether "memories hinder or help people in their effort to learn from the past and succeed in the present" (College Board, 2006, p. 3).

A speaker once told my high school class that the goldfish is the most unfortunate of creatures. His memory is so short-lived that when he is fed and happy he believes he has been happy all his life though when he is dying he cannot remember his happy times. He only believes that he has been dying his whole life. The speaker warned us—do not live like the goldfish. Remember all of your experiences, he told us. It is memory that can help you learn from the past. Memory is truly what sets us apart as rational beings. It is the only way to make amends with the past and succeed in the present. (College Board, 2006, p. 21).

The writer recounts a goldfish story and presents it as evidence that memory sets humans apart from other animals. But the reader would not know how the goldfish story is relevant to the writer's position unless the writer *tells* us. The second half of the excerpt connects the evidence to the position by "telling."

Students who have experienced "show, don't tell" already know a lot about presenting evidence. "Showing" is evidence. But in this case, the other half of the equation—"telling"— gets a new twist: If students learned there is power in *not telling* when they are writing certain kinds of narratives, now they learn that there is power in *telling* when they write arguments.

"Show, don't tell" becomes "show, then tell." It makes sense that if students are really steeped in one, it will be easier for them to cross the threshold to the other. Best of all, students discover they have something to bring to the task of argument. They are not blank slates, nor is writing an argument as daunting as they might have assumed.

Notching up the Task

> Spiraling occurs when students expand the
> number and kinds of things they can do well.

We have a friend who hates to move fast, especially in the early morning. He prefers to "taper into the day," as he puts it, by making coffee, glancing at the newspaper, and checking out the weather, first by peering through the window before he takes someone else's word for it. Too often students have no chance to taper. Instead of gentle (yet productive) moments to reflect on what they have learned or especially liked or wondered about, they are forced into moving rapidly from one thing to another, usually for the sake of standardization.

Our commitment is to helping our students develop intellectually, not to checking off skills as if they were items on a shopping list (or on a set of standards). By spiraling writing strategies, teachers can support student growth—even growth spurts—by weaving together past and present writing experiences, illustrated above in the first spiraling example. In this example, we add new stepped-up challenges.

It goes like this. One straightforward task for students is to write to people they know—teacher, peers, family members, friends—on a subject that's close to their hearts. So if students sit down to write to their parents for the purpose of persuading them to buy a new, improved smart phone, the best possible arguments are near at hand because students know the audience and situation. However, the argument takes on new dimensions when students have to write to people who are less familiar for a purpose that is a bit more removed, like writing to school board members for the purpose of persuading them to allow and even provide more, rather than fewer, electronic devices in classrooms and schools.

Recrafting information or arguments for various audiences and purposes means that students have to analyze different sets of circumstances. In this example, the advantage goes to the writer who can find the names of school board members and figure out what biases they may have, and what other, possibly more attractive expenditures they may be considering. In addition, a versatile writer would have a good grasp of the arguments for and against the use of various electronics on campus.

It's the savvy teacher who has helped students analyze the circumstances when the purpose and audience are closer to home and can then build on those lessons to expand the students' range of operation—a worthwhile spiraling technique. The expansion to unfamiliar territory makes it possible to work in the world.

That's why it's no surprise that the CCSS spotlight students' ability to adapt their writing in relation to audience, task, and purpose.

Creating a Connected Sequence of Assignments

Spiraling occurs when assignments or tasks build on each other.

Most teachers have some kind of scheme for rolling out their lessons. They use common sense. Some things come before others. And by itself, this could be sufficient. However, with the advent of any new reform effort like CCSS, someone else's monkey wrench (or idea of a hierarchy) is likely to get in the way.

Clearly, teachers want their students to learn new concepts and skills and become more accomplished at each one. However, one problematic interpretation of the CCSS is that students need to march in some linear fashion from one bump-up to the next. Not only would that be a misinterpretation, it would be detrimental to students and, yes, to their teachers as well. Think instead about how assignments might interrelate and how they might add to what Moffett (1981) calls an "accumulating repertory" for students (p. 10). When Moffett created his idea of a sequence of assignments, he designated a definite set of progressions. One moves from familiar, close-to-home audiences and subjects to those that are less familiar and more distant. The other moves from recording what is happening (interior monologues, drama) to recording what happened (narrative, diaries) to generalizing (informational writing or exposition) to inferring what will, may, or could be true (logical argumentation).

But instead of plowing ahead on a one-way street, these writing dimensions and tasks build on each other. Nothing is ever really dropped, even as new genres are added. Students might write dialogues on one occasion, for example, and a later assignment might explicitly invite dialogue in a narrative or informational piece of writing.

In Moffett's world, young writers are allowed to dip into unfamiliar water one foot at a time. For example, suppose there is a mishap in the school cafeteria or at one of the lunchtime service areas. Perhaps it is a bad food day or a slow-moving line that keeps students from getting their snacks or drinks before the next class. Writing about this incident in narrative form is a first dip. But the experience has a longer shelf life. According to Moffett (1965), any subject like this one "may be abstracted to any level" (p. 244). The next dip might be an informational piece in which "the cafeteria scene will become a mere example, among several others, of some general statement such as 'The food you get in restaurants is not as good as what you get at home'"(p. 245). And that ubiquitous cafeteria incident could also serve as one piece of evidence in an argument for an open campus at lunchtime. In other words, "every authentic writing activity can be done at many levels of maturity" (Moffett, 1981, p. 13).

This is an example of the way Moffett interweaves progressions. But progression does "*not* mean that formal or more impersonal or more abstract writing is better. The goal of writing through such a spectrum is not to 'come out on top' but to be able to play the whole range" (Moffett, 1981, p. 12).

Taking Reading to the Next Level

> Spiraling occurs when students encounter increasingly sophisticated reading for increasingly sophisticated purposes.

One important influence on the writers of the CCSS was a study conducted by American College Testing (ACT, 2007) that showed that "Just over half of our students are able to meet the demands of college-level reading, based on ACT's national readiness indicator" (p. 2). The determining factor in college readiness was students' ability to comprehend complex texts.

So the mantra has become "complexity."

If we asked people on the street to name the hardest thing they have to read, we would surely get different answers. One person might say "my tax return." Another might identify the bus or train schedule. And every parent who has tried to decipher instructions for assembling a toy could legitimately nominate this kind of reading as difficult and also annoying. For the academically oriented reader, the answer might be something like *War and Peace*. And for anyone of us, perhaps one of the toughest reading experiences is online research, for example, looking up some health issue. In this instance, the reader has to negotiate terminology, conflicting opinions, and dense ideas or information *plus* figure out the trustworthiness of the sources. The point is that complexity is not just one thing. There is no one simple way to account for it.

What's more, not all the current measures of text complexity are necessarily helpful. Without a doubt, teachers are likely to run smack into lexicons—measures that count things like linking words or clauses in a sentence or number of syllables in a word. But the question is: Is that all there is to complexity?

Chall, Bissex, Conard, and Harris-Sharples (1999) argue that a strictly quantitative view of text complexity is limited (not to mention cumbersome). Qualitative measures, on the other hand, are more sensitive to the wide variety of elements that differentiate easy texts from hard ones. Putting the quantitative and qualitative together might look like this:

- Language—vocabulary difficulty
- Sentence length and complexity
- Conceptual difficulty—the degree of abstractness; the amount of prior knowledge needed to understand a text
- Idea density and difficulty—the number of ideas in the text and the difficulty of these ideas (Chall et al., 1999)

This list is especially useful when it comes to selecting reading in the disciplines where so much depends on conceptual understanding. Suppose we were sitting in a chemistry class with our English language arts brains frozen in terror. Out comes the first reading. Suddenly we are being asked to understand thermodynamics or photochemical reactions. And even if we grasp some part of the content, will we be able to do anything with it?

Learning the concepts of a discipline—being able to understand and use the ideas, whether in conversation or in writing—is a primary concern of Arthur Applebee (2002): "If students are to participate effectively in a domain, they must learn how to take action within that domain: how to *do* science, for example, not simply to learn *about* it" (p. 105). Applebee explains that students need knowledge of content "in order to partake in the ongoing conversation about significant ideas" (p. 106).

When it comes down to it, then, teachers might best select texts with a "do something" in mind. As with our other examples of spiraling, the reading and the "do something" will build on and expand what has come before.

Considerations for Selecting and Using Texts. Here are some practical suggestions:

- Select texts that are important to you and your students and that complement what you are trying to teach. Don't be bullied into using a complex text for complexity's sake. Don't drown in lexicons.
- Consider what your students already know about a given topic or what you will teach them in advance as groundwork. Students will be more prepared to take on complex texts if they have some prior knowledge.
- Students should engage in increasingly complex texts. But be sure to consider how you will use the texts. You can present less complicated texts when you are introducing complicated concepts or when you are asking students to perform complicated tasks.
- Select texts that represent good writing and interesting subject matter worthy of intensive study.
- Plan how students will read the text. Reading aloud to students may make more room for significantly challenging texts.

Perhaps the hardest thing about selecting a text is finding one that will engage a wide range of students, including both males and females, as well as students from a variety of cultural backgrounds. With a single text like a novel, a primary consideration is the extent to which the book deals with relevant, exciting, and challenging topics. For example, Kelly Gallagher (2009) points out the value in teaching *To Kill a Mockingbird*:

[It is] not simply to provide our students with a slice of cultural literacy or to teach them to recognize literary elements such as foreshadowing. The value comes when we use this great book as a springboard to examine issues in today's world. . . . teaching *To Kill a Mockingbird* provides the modern student the opportunity to examine racism in their world. (pp. 66–67)

Reading at its Best. Students benefit from learning to read at all levels—from reading that comes easily to reading that takes more work. As with writing, the goal is for students to be accomplished readers across a range of reading. It would be a disservice to students to throw out the variety of reading that advances both their skills at dealing with more complicated material and their enjoyment of reading. Kelly Gallagher (2009) puts it this way:

> To mix up the reading diet of my students, I want half of their reading to be academic, and I want half of their reading to be recreational. By emphasizing recreational reading, I am not underselling the value of academic texts . . . reading difficult text is essential and plays an important role in developing young readers (and young citizens). But students who read only academic texts become students who never read recreational texts. That is unconscionable. (p. 82)

Buried in the CCSS Appendix A is a statement that supports Gallagher's view: "Students need opportunities to stretch their reading abilities but also to experience the satisfaction of easy, fluent reading"(CCSSO & NGA, 2010, p. 9).

Exactly.

DIVING DEEPER:
SPIRALING, SCAFFOLDING, AND SCRIMMAGING

Together spiraling and scaffolding put learning within reach of students;
scrimmages give students repeated, manageable practice.

Spiraling and scaffolding. They're like fish and chips, peanut butter and jelly, steak and fries. They go together, and together they make it possible to take on adult-sized tasks like playing basketball long before children are 6 feet tall and coordinated enough to dribble down the court.

When it comes to scaffolding, coaches know how to put players through their paces. Coaches break things down (dribbling, pivoting, passing, shooting), teach the plays, set up scrimmages (practice games), and then turn the kids loose to play the real game (with a lot of shouting from the sidelines). Good writing teachers do the same.

Whether on the court or in the classroom, scaffolding is short-lived (learners and players don't need scaffolding forever). Its goal is to grease the wheels, easing learners/players into becoming independently good at something.

The CCSS stress independent performance as the end goal. However, this does not in any way negate the need for scaffolding. We might say that teaching is scaffolding or, conversely, scaffolding is teaching. Either way, it's all about building bridges for students so that ultimately they can do things on their own.

Case Study: Writing Scrimmages and Other Manageable Practices

During her long career as a teacher and teacher educator, Rebekah Caplan developed the idea of writing scrimmages (little workouts or minitasks). The hallmarks of a writing scrimmage are (1) its length (one paragraph, no more than two), (2) its focus on practicing a particular strategy, and (3) the idea that students share their short bursts of writing and get feedback. The value, according to Caplan: "It's a chance for students to practice developing an idea in a short frame, and a chance for me as a teacher to practice instruction on manageable pieces of writing" (unless cited otherwise, all Caplan quotes in this chapter are from a personal communication, December 9, 2013).

Take the often-taught writing strategy of comparison/contrast. Rather than assigning a full-blown paper right off the bat, Caplan sets up a workable situation in which students can try out a complex thinking strategy. She also assures that the topic itself doesn't get in the way by choosing something familiar, for example, "Saturday is different from Sunday." Here's how an 11th-grader responded:

> Without the help of an alarm clock, at 8:30 sharp Saturday morning, I wake up brimmed with energy and ready to take on any activity that floats my way. The sun is pouring bars of golden liquid in my window and the blue jays are singing merrily at the top of their musical voices. Anticipating a whole day to do whatever I want, I eagerly throw on my clothes and spring down the stairs. After a light breakfast I grab my old familiar cut-offs and my favorite beach towel, jump in the convertible, and with a delightful screech of the wheels, fly off to spend a beautiful day running and laughing in the sun.
>
> My mother is shaking me and saying, "It's past 11:00. Get up; there's work to do." With a deep groan I open my bloodshot eyes and am immediately blinded by the terrible glare of the sun beaming hot and stuffy directly on me. Very slowly I claw my way out of bed, and in a drained, limp state of semi-consciousness, stumble sheepishly down the stairs. My family, faces cheerful and repulsive, is having breakfast. Just the aroma of eggs turns my stomach, making me feel queasy. Instead, I trudge to the cabinet, fumble with a bottle of aspirin, and with a glass of warm water sloppily gulp three down. Then, still hungover and depressed, I sit down and stare straight ahead, thinking about the agony of mowing the lawn. (Caplan, 1984, pp. 56–57)

Once students have practiced comparing familiar objects, people, places, and events, Caplan moves into new territory where students tackle more complex tasks with less homespun topics. In the example that follows, this 11th-grader responds to the prompt "Though Fitzgerald's and Hemingway's stories start out similarly, they end up rather differently."

> *The Great Gatsby* and *The Sun Also Rises* start at the same point and end up with two different solutions to a problem which is virtually the same. Both men, Jay Gatsby and Jake Barnes, have a dependency problem on a woman whom they cannot have. Upon finally coming to grips with this reality, Gatsby is destroyed while Jake grows within himself. The drastically different endings seem to indicate that Fitzgerald felt that it was wrong to hold onto an unattainable dream for so long, and that only disaster could stem from staring at one "green beacon" and ignoring the rest of one's life. Hemingway shared this idea, but expressed that it was never too late to change, and that after you have made all your mistakes and stumbled in ignorance, the sun also rises, and there is a new day in which new opportunities can be found. (Caplan, 1984, p. 64)

Note that Caplan has used the scrimmages to teach students two different organizational schemes for comparing and contrasting. In the first instance, the writer devotes one paragraph to Saturday's activities and one paragraph to Sunday's. This is often the more familiar route. As Caplan advances the sophistication of the topics, she teaches students another construction—interweaving the comparisons in one paragraph.

More About Scrimmages

Sometimes it matters where scrimmages live. Caplan suggests that students keep a notebook of their reading and writing exercises so they can return periodically to strengthen or expand them. In effect, the notebook becomes a place where students build capacity.

Some of Caplan's notebook scrimmages for learning more about argument appear in Figure 4.1.

Note the variety of writing scrimmages. Some specify the rhetorical move, for example, adding a quotation to support an argument or explaining the relevance of a statistic. Others offer a sentence frame for students to "try on" as a way to integrate or explain evidence. And still another invites students to adopt another persona in order to explore a counterargument. In every case, Caplan carefully teaches the strategy—including close examination of models—before asking students to jump into a scrimmage.

A word of caution about sentence frames: "I always worry about static use of sentence frames," says Caplan. "The list of sentence frames needs to grow and grow. It needs to be an organic and dynamic list. Students can help add to the sentence frames as they find them in new texts, hear them on the news, or from each other."

Figure 4.1. Writing Scrimmages for Argument

Show that you can

- Add an anecdote, fact, statistic, quotation, question that represents why the topic is of importance
- Explain the relevance of an anecdote, fact, statistic, quotation, question, graphic, illustration, and so on
- State a claim in light of a counterclaim:
  - » It is understandable that . . . however . . . as a result . . .
  - » Although . . . it is also true that . . . therefore . . .
  - » Admittedly . . . nevertheless . . . so . . .
  - » Despite the fact that . . . one needs to also consider . . . in short . . .
- Integrate textual evidence to explain information and/or emphasize a point, citing sources accurately:
  - » _____ (author) in _____ (source information) explains/describes/predicts/argues/claims/asserts "_____"
  - » According to _____ in _____, "_____"
  - » Research conducted by _____ on _____ suggests that "_____"
- Follow with an explanation that interprets the evidence:
  - » This statement/explanation/finding, emphasizes _____, supports _____, makes the case for_____, calls into question_____
- Explain the logic behind a viewpoint that is not your own:
  - » Pretend you believe an opposing viewpoint and need to explain it to someone else. Try to convince someone to agree with you.

The Value of Practice

Is there a magic number of hours someone has to practice to become a world-class expert at something? The idea that excellence at performing a complex task requires a critical minimum level of practice surfaces again and again in studies of expertise. In fact, researchers have settled on what they believe is the magic number for true expertise: 10,000 hours.

> "The emerging picture from such studies is that ten thousand hours of practice is required to achieve the level of mastery associated with being a world-class expert—in anything," writes neurologist Daniel Levitin. "In study after study, of composers, basketball players, fiction writers, ice skaters, concert pianists, chess players, master criminals, and what have you, this number comes up again and again. Of course, this doesn't address why some people get more out of their practice sessions than others do. But no one has yet found a case in which true world-class expertise was accomplished in less time. It seems that it takes the brain this long to assimilate all that it needs to know to achieve true mastery. (Levitin, quoted in Gladwell, 2008, p. 40)

Malcolm Gladwell's (2008) story of Bill Gates provides an example. Not surprisingly, little Bill was a precocious child and somewhat bored in school. So at the start of 7th grade his parents sent him to a private school near his home in Seattle. Sometime around his 2nd year at Lakeside, the school launched a computer club. Most universities didn't even have computer clubs in the late 1960s. As the story goes, Bill Gates began doing real-time programming in the 8th grade.

That was the beginning of a lifetime love affair with computers. Bill Gates took up residence in the computer room where he and other students taught themselves the wonders of this new technology. After school Gates programmed until the wee hours. Gates and his friends also began hanging out at the University of Washington's computer center and arranged to get free computer time from a group called ISI (Information Sciences Inc.). In one 7-month stretch Gates and friends used up 1,575 hours of computer time—the equivalent of eight hours a day, seven days a week.

The story goes on and on. Gates used the computers at the University of Washington every morning between 3:00 and 6:00. "By the time Gates dropped out of Harvard after his sophomore year to try his hand at his own software company, he'd been programming practically nonstop for seven consecutive years. He was *way* past ten thousand hours" (pp. 54–55).

We recount this story to emphasize that practice means more to success than anyone might guess, especially students who might think of practice as drudgery. Of course we don't envision most students giving 10,000 hours to writing. But it's an eye-opener for students to think about the relationship between practice, learning, and becoming an expert at something. Teachers might ask students to select something they do that takes a lot of practice. In a quick-write ask them to explain how long they are willing to practice; what keeps them practicing; and what effect they think practice has on their performance. Then gently (but not too gently) point out that practice is also part of getting better at writing. Scaffolding for writing includes lots and lots of practice.

CAPTURING THE BIG IDEA OF SCAFFOLDING

While it's true that young students (and old ones too) need scaffolding to make strides in their learning, there are lots of questions still up for grabs: when, what kind, how much, and for how long? Lev Vygotsky had a theory that puts some sensible markers around scaffolding. His famous *zone of proximal development* (ZPD) refers to the territory between what a student can do without help from others and what he or she can do with help, or as Vygotsky (1978) put it, "the distance between the actual developmental level as determined by independent problem solving and the level of potential development as determined through problem solving under adult guidance, or in collaboration with more capable peers" (p. 86). Although he never used the term *scaffolding*, "Vygotsky believed that when a student is at the ZPD for a particular task, providing the appropriate assistance will give the student enough of a 'boost' to achieve the task" (McLeod, 2012, para. 3). "Appropriate assistance" is scaffolding, pure and simple.

Over time and through necessity, teachers have invented dozens of ways to scaffold. Several years ago, we visited Newcomer High School in San Francisco, where newly arrived immigrant high school students spend their 1st year in this country learning to speak, read, and write enough English to move on to a regular high school program. We sat in classroom after classroom where teachers pulled out every stop to teach English and other subjects—from miming and role playing, to modeling and illustrating, to using props, word walls, and pictures.

TAKING THE PLUNGE:
POSSIBILITIES FOR SCAFFOLDING

Scaffolding techniques are seemingly inexhaustible. We have listed a few in Figure 4.2, but of course lists do not reveal anything about which approaches work best on what occasions. The smart money, when it comes to scaffolding, is on writing itself. As a tool for generating or thinking out ideas or for trying out new features or skills, writing can't be beat. Writing about content boosts students' overall learning as well (Bangert-Drowns, Hurley, & Wilkinson, 2004; Graham & Perin, 2007). And the more students learn about the subject of their writing, the better they are likely to do.

Figure 4.2. Some Ways to Scaffold Writing

- Keeping notebooks
- Modeling
- Practicing with short pieces
- Collaborating
- Breaking things down
- Zeroing in on certain features, structures, or skills
- Working on one chunk at a time
- Mapping/drawing
- Discussing with partners/groups/whole class
- Identifying audience and purpose
- Tapping into prior knowledge
- Building content knowledge
- Teaching vocabulary
- Improvising/role playing
- Using visuals
- Writing itself!

88 Uncommonly Good Ideas

The following case study begins with a premise about scaffolding: A surefire way to determine "when, what kind, how much, and for how long" is to try out your own assignment. Write that paper yourself. What you learn will be the basis for your scaffolding.

Case Study: Scaffolding Research for English Language Learners

Tracey Freyre teaches English language learners at a multi-ethnic high school in California, including students in 9th-grade Intensive English whose reading levels fall below grade 6. Students take on the same kinds of assignments and skills they will encounter in their "regular" English class but with extra support.

Since research is one of the key requirements at the high school, Freyre has it on the front burner for the intensive students. Together with two colleagues from two other high schools in the district, Beth Gabow and Patricia Riek, Freyre developed a second semester project that asked students to research a particular member of the Little Rock Nine in order to answer this question: "*What was ____'s experience with the Little Rock Nine and how did integrating Central High School impact his or her life?*"

Freyre, Gabow, and Riek talked first about what they wanted the final piece to look like and back-mapped from there. Then came the ultimate test. They tried out their own assignment to determine the steps in the process and to determine where students would encounter roadblocks.

Scaffolding is the heart and soul of Freyre's ELL teaching and of this 18-day unit. Here are some of the scaffolding techniques.

Modeling. The teachers created an example text about a member of the Little Rock Nine. In sharing the model with their students, they pointed out what each paragraph accomplished in terms of content, options for writing an introduction (anecdote, statistic, questions), and the increasing specificity within paragraphs.

"To find out where the bumps are in a task, do it yourself." (JoAnne Eresh, personal communication, February 5, 2001)

Context Building. Many of Freyre's students had never heard of the civil rights movement, although they had come across Martin Luther King, a person they thought to be a slave. To set the scene and to get students interested and invested, Freyre spent a week building background, beginning with a slide show of famous images from the civil rights movement. "Starting with visuals rather than reading was a big key to how students would ultimately receive a text. By the time they began their reading, they were so fascinated that the room was absolutely silent" (all Freyre quotes are from a personal communication, February 1, 2014).

Content Building. The teachers assigned students a member of the Little Rock Nine as their subject. Those who had the same person sat together and shared what they were learning in their research. To ensure that students amassed enough relevant content, teachers provided research questions for each paragraph.

Breaking Things Down. Students researched, wrote, and revised their papers paragraph by paragraph, using the computer lab a day or two at a time. "For these students, it would have been difficult to draft the whole thing at once, day after day. But tackling it in chunks gave students the stamina to stay focused and the benefit of seeing accomplishment at each step."

Another way Freyre worked with chunks was to focus on certain parts of the writing task, for example, the conclusion. Figure 4.3 (on the following page) presents the kinds of questions that helped students draft the last paragraph of their essays.

Zeroing in on Bugaboos. Freyre taught her students to choose a good quote that supported their point (not hard for students, she said). "The harder part of the job is how to add their own original ideas about the quote." To help with this hurdle, Freyre taught them to focus on a particular phrase or word in the quotation as the thing to analyze. For example, in a sentence about life inside an integrated school—*some racist teachers simply ignored their Black students*—the spotlight might shine on the word *ignore*. Why would someone ignore? What would that mean?

Determining Structure. One way Freyre helped students with structure was to specify content for various paragraphs: After the introductory paragraph, students devoted the second paragraph to historical background, the third to the person's experience as a member of the Little Rock Nine, the fourth to the impact of the experience, and the final paragraph to the relevance of the experience to the world today. While five paragraphs in length, this particular marriage of content and structure goes beyond the typical "what and three whys" formula.

Collaborating. Freyre's students collaborated on building content, on reading each other's draft paragraphs, on determining if the information was sufficient, and on figuring out whether the information relied too heavily on the text and not enough on the student writer's own words.

And how did all this careful scaffolding make a difference? "We were impressed with the quality of the work compared with previous years," Freyre said. "The students were more invested and engaged, and they were

Figure 4.3. Scaffolding a Conclusion

What was your person's major contribution to the Little Rock Nine?	
How are public schools in the United States different today because of the Little Rock Nine?	
What types of discrimination do students still face today?	
What lessons do the Little Rock Nine teach people about addressing discrimination today?	

proud of themselves. They told us in their reflections that they learned a lot and that the project was hard, but not too hard."

Student Writing. A quick glance at the essay below shows that the writer has a good amount of content. The paper is long., It's not measured in inches. There is meat on the bones, so to speak, the payoff of Freyre's careful scaffolding.

Minnijean Brown: The War for Peace

by Isabel Barajas

Before the Brown v. Board of Education, there was segregation. The black schools were inferior from the white schools because the blacks had broken down buildings and outdated books and the whites had schools with heating and updated books (Peters, Jennifer L. "The Case That Rocked Education Brown v. Board of Education"). African Americans responded to segregation in the schools by making a Supreme Court case called Brown V. Board of Education. The Brown V. Board is a case that ended segregation and began integrating schools. The case of the Brown V. Board of Education's outcome was making a law to stop segregation and start integrating the white and black schools. The Little Rock Nine, the nine black students, integrated a white high school in 1957, because they wanted to stop racism and get better education so they can get good jobs when they graduate and get accepted in good colleges. Minnijean Brown was a member of the Little Rock Nine. Integrating Central high school was difficult and stressful for her, and the

> Para. 1.
> Establishes the context for Minnijean Brown and the Little Rock Nine. Cites source. Explains or defines key titles and terms: Brown V. Board, Little Rock Nine, activist.

experience made her become an activist, a person who fights for rights and causes.

Minnijean Brown was born on September 11, 1941, in Little Rock, Arkansas. Minnijean Brown was the oldest out of four children. Minnijean's mother worked as a nurse and a homemaker, and her father worked as a landscaping contractor and an independent mason. Minnijean is the sister of Bobby Brown who was the president of Black United Youth in the 1960's. The article Unsung Heroines states "This trial by fire was just Minnijean's first step on the path of social and political activism, she's gone on to fight for minority rights and environmental justice both here and in Canada" (Minnijean Brown Trickey, Environmental and Civil Rights Activist). One of the reasons Minnijean Brown joined the Little Rock Nine is because she wanted to end segregation and she didn't like the conditions of segregation.

> Para. 2. Situates Minnijean Brown in time, place, and family relationships.

Minnijean Brown's experience as a member of the Little Rock Nine was difficult because she was bullied and called names because she was black. When Minnijean Brown became a member of the Little Rock Nine she started getting death threats. The article states, "As one of the Little Rock Nine, she along with eight other Black American teenagers, defied death threats, hostile white demonstrators, and even the Arkansas national guards, to attend the all-white Little Rock Central high 1957" (Minnijean Brown Trickey (b.1941) Civil Right Activist Who Integrated Central High School in 1957). Minnijean Brown and the other eight were bullied and threatened and called names because of their race. Since the Little Rock Nine were a different race from the whites, they were taunted and teased for going to a white school. When Minnijean Brown entered the Central High School, some whites were screaming mean things that scared Minnijean Brown. Minnijean Brown states "I remember feeling very scared and people were screaming obscenities, like 'go back to Africa' and 'integrate is communism' and all kinds of crazy stuff like that" (Minnijean Brown Trickey, Environmental and Civil Rights Activist). Minnijean Brown felt like the whites didn't want her in the country or state because she was a different race so the whites were saying to her to go back to Africa even though she was born in the United States. Minnijean Brown never experienced white people calling her names and telling her they will kill her. Minnijean Brown as a member of the Little Rock Nine ignored the mean things people said and later became an activist a person who fights for rights and causes.

> Para. 3. Cites sources, uses quotes, details, and description to depict the risky nature of Minnijean's experience.

Minnijean Brown became an activist, so that she can try to stop racism and help African Americans be treated the same way whites were treated. When Minnijean Brown became an activist she later became someone who worked for the president. After Minnijean Brown graduated from New York Lincoln School she became a social activist and she worked for the Clinton administration as deputy assistant secretary (Minnijean Brown the Little Rock Nine Foundation). Minnijean Brown didn't want others to be bullied and taunted and teased like she was, because she was different so she became an activist to help people who want to be treated the same way others treat their family and friends. Minnijean Brown wants people to find their common ground and think about what they're saying and doing. The article states "she asked all people to 'find their common ground', don't tell me how different we are and to learn and practice the values of non-violence" (Minnijean Brown Trickey (1941). Minnijean Brown wants people to be non-violent and act friendly to others. Minnijean doesn't want people to judge others because there different she wants them to understand how everyone is the same. Minnijean Brown wants to stop people who are getting bullied and teased, she wants others not to feel the same way she felt when she got bullied and teased, Minnijean wants to show even though you seem different from others you can be treated in a respectful way.

> Para. 4 Uses facts, quotations and explanations to convey the aftermath of Minnijean's participation in integrating Central High and its impact on her beliefs.

Minnijean's major contribution to the little Rock Nine is to fight back because sometimes you can't let people hurt you and call you names. When Minnijean got called names at by a boy she fought back by pouring a bowl of chili on him, when a girl bullied Minnijean she fought back by calling her white trash. Today there is still discrimination in schools because I myself witnessed some guy calling his friend gay for doing something he didn't like his friend doing. The types of discrimination students face today are getting bullied because you're gay or bisexual or lesbian, some discrimination is based on looks or how students dress differently from other people around them. The lessons the Little Rock Nine teach was for people to not be racist and not to judge others for who they are. If we can learn these lessons, we can live in a better society that is respectful.

> Para. 5. Uses examples to illustrate discrimination in the 1950s and in the writer's school today. Summarizes the lesson of the Little Rock Nine.

Thoughts About Taking Time for Content

The writer of this piece packs in a lot of information because her teacher devoted hours to establishing the essential ingredients for a successful essay. While it's true there are some redundancies, the fact remains that the student has a grasp on her subject and its historical significance—content knowledge that gives her writing some muscle and heft. Had she tried to write with only bits of information, the result could have been far different. According to Judith Langer (1984):

> When students have few ideas about a topic, or when they are unwilling to risk stating the ideas they do have, their writing may rely on glib generalizations, unsupported by argument or enriching illustrations. At other times when their knowledge is fragmentary, their writing may become little more than a list of vaguely associated items of information with few explicit connections among the ideas. (pp. 28–29)

One More Note About Scaffolding

Scaffolding is not reserved for special cases, such as ELL students, students with special needs, or the very young. All students benefit from scaffolding, especially when they are attempting demanding tasks or learning new techniques.

DIVING DEEPER:
SCAFFOLDING FOR WRITING FROM READING

Like most teachers, Deborah Appleman recognizes that plot summaries too often take up the bulk of a literary analysis. She recommends pushing students up the inferential ladder toward interpretation and evaluation by locating the assignments more squarely in their world. She suggests finding audiences other than the teacher and purposes other than telling the teacher what she or he already knows.

> "The biggest stretch for students is moving from the book report to a critical piece on a book." Barbara Buckley (personal communication, January 23, 2013)

Case Study: Scaffolding Literary Analysis

"No living 14-year-old can write anything about a book like Huck Finn that hasn't been written before or that can't be found on the Internet." So says Deborah Appleman, former high school teacher and now Hollis L. Caswell Professor of Educational Studies at Carleton College, Minnesota (all Appleman quotes are from a personal communication, March 10, 2014). For Appleman, scaffolding for literary analysis is about revisiting purpose and audience:

> When we ask students to report on a book and what happens and what was the main conflict, we prevent young writers from moving

up the inferential ladder. They end up summarizing the plot for an audience who knows it all too well: the teacher.

Appleman sees the purpose of literary analysis as reading and writing to try to make significance or meaning. "Reading literature helps us talk to kids about things that mean something to them, that mirror real-life experiences." What's more, with the increased role of nonfiction in the English curriculum, Appleman believes it's important to expand our notion of literary analysis to include, for example, analyzing a billboard, an Oscar acceptance speech, or the Emancipation Proclamation. "We need to apply the tools of literary analysis to nonfiction and other kinds of texts," says Appleman. She offers several suggestions.

Use an Organic Jumping-off Place. Literary analysis is social and contextual. One platform for writing, then, is a class discussion. Imagine picking up some of the important threads of the group conversation—questions or quotations—and then asking students to extend one of them into a piece of writing. Students might examine the unexpected ending of the book or look at some kind of frame in which the book exists. What does it tell us about the world we live in or about social classes or gender issues? "We can help students veer away from formulas by moving them organically from a conversation they just had together to writing about their reading."

Change the Writing Situation. "People have written a million essays about Huck Finn and they've bought a lot of them online too," Appleman points out. But if students use the book to understand a real-life event, they are no longer in a position of searching the Internet to find the right answer for the right teacher. "Students can speculate about the kind of relationship Huck and Jim had by examining how friendship and understanding can occur between people of different backgrounds, and then applying their ideas to a recent happening at school or to a more global event," suggests Appleman. She also recommends decontextualizing the characters: *Huck and Jim are walking around a shopping mall on a busy Saturday afternoon. They simultaneously spot a wallet containing $100 in cash. What will each of them want to do and why? Support with evidence from the text.* In these examples, modifying the writing situation actually ratchets up the typical literary analysis paper. Students move away from telling what they know to someone who knows more. Instead, they apply what they know in a different context.

Find More Authentic Audiences and Purposes. "It's hard for students to have an authentic voice when they're spitting into the wind," Appleman notes. By this, she is referring to whether students find the purpose and audience for their writing to be clear and relevant. For example, if students write to a friend or friends—whether in a letter or blog post or some other form—for the purpose of convincing them why they should or should not read a certain book, the writing is no longer disembodied. What's more, the writers have to come to grips with some classic features of analysis—examining the reason for reading in the first place, along with their own criteria for what constitutes a good book. Teachers can escalate this scenario by plugging in a more distant audience and a different kind of task: The school board has only enough money for one set of books. Which book should it be and why? Whether students write a letter or a speech, they face the need to articulate criteria for literary quality.

Appleman wants students to consider multiple texts/themes/ideas and how they intersect. By including one or two poems or a newspaper article with the selected book, teachers engage their students in tasks that fall into the category of academic writing and that also mimic what readers do when they read—make connections to other readings, movies, TV shows, personal experiences, world events, and so on.

DIVING IN AGAIN:
LEARNING TO WORK WITH MULTIPLE TEXTS

Scaffolding is like rehearsing for a play. It takes a lot more time than the ultimate performance.

Here's an insider tip about academic writing assignments in college: typically they ask students to work with more than one text at a time and, in some way, to bring those texts together in a "conversation." Some possible analogies are a family dinner table or a formal panel where a "moderator" has the job of finding points of agreement and disagreement, of weighing each of them, and, in the case of an argument, of moving the audience/family members in a certain direction. Now translate "moderator" to "writer of an academic essay." But where can a young writer find a model for this kind of intellectual activity? Anyone who has viewed a political show on cable TV knows that everyone shouts and no one listens. How can a high school student rise above the everyday barrage of talking heads and engage instead reasoned, well-researched ideas that take into account other opinions?

We turn to California State University–Chico Professor Tom Fox for some strategies that will give secondary students a leg up. Fox recommends helping students find out how to link ideas across multiple texts and how to weave those ideas into a coherent argument about an issue of significance.

Of course, we're not suggesting that every secondary teacher has to emulate the exact requirements of a college academic essay. Rather, we hope the steps Fox has developed will give students in middle and high school the very tools they will need when they do encounter that conversation among texts.

Case Study: Integrating Ideas from Multiple Texts

Tom Fox knows what to expect when his 1st-year composition students arrive at CSU Chico. They definitely have opinions, but their grasp of all the complexities of a given issue is often limited. And that's not all. Their strategy for using sources when making an argument is to scour whatever is available in support of their initial position or idea. It's no surprise, then, that they are in a less powerful position than their sources. Indeed, their sources get the upper hand as the embattled writers pack their pieces with quotes and then simply parrot what the "experts" just said. Fox wants his student writers to be the authorities, and one way for them to do that is to commandeer their sources.

At the outset, Fox invites students to come up with their own topics, something they care about, something, too, that is an issue of common concern. From there, Fox directs them to what scholars and writers are saying about their topic by helping them find sources, particularly those that provide alternative points of view. An important thing happens: Students immerse themselves in research that's coming from many directions (as opposed to taking a one-way road by reading only sources that agree with their own position).

This is the moment when students can actually make a claim worth claiming, although Fox notes it is not yet set in stone. With initial claim in hand, students write a proposal that encompasses background, research, proposed project, benefits of considering this issue, audience, timeline of work, and bibliography of sources. Each proposal gets a number to ensure an impartial response by one of the class review boards. "I organize the class into groups of three and each group gets three proposals to review. Each person is responsible for leading the discussion and for writing a response to the author of one of the proposals based on the group's discussion. The review boards give the class a sense of high expectations," says Fox. "The process lets students know they need to get in gear" (all Fox quotes are from a personal communication, February 27, 2014).

It's not hard to imagine that students emerge from this kind of intensive scaffolding with more authority. But the next step is translating that authority into their essays. From day 1, Fox teaches students an alternative to simply dropping a quote into the piece. "I tell them they need to give the reader a stronger idea of why they are using the quote. We work on signal phrases, that is, phrases that signal 'here's a quote.' We want signal phrases with content, not just signal phrases that say 'according to.'"

Here's the difference:

Signal Phrase Without Content. Li Mingqi, who was working in the management part of Foxconn Technology, said, "Apple never cared about anything other than increasing product quality and decreasing production cost."

Signal Phrase with Content. Li Mingqi, who was working as management in Foxconn Technology, notes that Apple ignored working conditions: "Apple never cared about anything other than increasing product quality and decreasing production cost."

One important take-away from this case study is the amount of time Fox takes to front-load the writing of an argument and the depth of his scaffolding. While end products matter, the real teaching is in the getting-there. In Fox's case, students write an argument and then remix it into a multimedia production (TED Talk, webpage, Prezi). Students present their projects to an audience of friends, parents, community members, faculty, and so forth—an activity that Fox enjoys but doesn't overplay. "I want them to learn some new technology, and sometimes it fails." What doesn't fail is Fox's approach to scaffolding and the way he defines for his students their newfound expertise: "I call it knowing a lot more than the average person on the street."

LAST THOUGHTS

Both Fox and Appleman suggest that writing *about* reading is a limited pursuit. Doing something *with* the reading connects purpose, audience, and content in a way that engages students and, we hope, gives them an authoritative voice. It's a theme that extends to the CCSS. Students are to use what they read in print or online as a source from which to "draw evidence . . . to support analysis, reflection, and research" (CCSS & NGA, p. 44).

It's no easy thing for students to sort through, verify, paraphrase, quote from, and otherwise dive actively into their sources for evidence. If the thinking behind spiraling is to move learning upward and outward, then students need as many tools as teachers can give them to get better at reading and writing, the kind of tools the students can turn to when the going gets rough.

We know a teacher who decided, after her students finished a particularly difficult assignment as homework, to survey them on what strategies they used to draft their ideas and to inch forward when they got stuck. Did you go back and read what you had already written to spur on your next thoughts, she asked. Did you review your notes or return to a particular section of your reading? Did you walk away from your desk or computer and talk to someone about your fledgling ideas? The students answered no to each question. And in fact, they had trouble articulating exactly what they did do to get to the end.

This teacher was a good detective. She suspected her students had not soaked in all the scaffolding techniques she had introduced. As students sometimes do, they left their learning in the classroom rather than taking it with them. For scaffolding to work, students have to be able to retrieve the right technique at the right moment in their writing, even without the teacher.

Scaffolding, like all learning, is meant to be portable, to leave the classroom in the backpacks and brains of students where it can be fetched or recalled at any time. It is meant to be plentiful—a whole toolkit of techniques. One or two ready-to-wear pieces of scaffolding will not be suitable for all occasions. And it is meant to boost competence, resourcefulness, and independence—for the times when students have to go it alone. The more teachers and students talk intentionally about scaffolding—"what do we call this strategy and how did it help you?"—the more likely students will become the owners.

CHAPTER 5

Collaborating

You might wonder when you pick up the CCSS anchor standards for writing what happened to face-to-face collaboration. It seems that where the writing standards are concerned, collaboration is a strictly digital affair: "Use technology, including the Internet, to produce and publish writing and to interact and collaborate with others" (CCSSO & NGA, 2010, p. 41). But stay tuned. If you flip to the speaking and listening anchor standards, you find another, perhaps more human-centered idea of collaboration:

> Prepare for and participate effectively in a range of conversations and collaborations with diverse partners, building on other's ideas and expressing their [students'] own clearly and persuasively. (CCSSO & NGA, 2010, p. 48)

Wherever it shows up in the CCSS, collaboration appears at all points on the compass in the process of writing, from generating ideas to responding to drafts. It's critical to learning to write because students do not do as well in solitary confinement as they do when they can compare and share. In fact, by collaborating, students bump up against the idea of audience—not just once, but over and over again. At the point they talk about their papers, for example, they quickly find out they aren't writing simply to please themselves. Readers are a big deal. If readers don't understand what's going on in the paper, the writer needs to know why. That's something a reader can tell them. Eventually, and as a result of lots of collaborative experiences, writers carry around a reader in their heads, making it easier to spot glitches and gaps in their own work.

In this chapter, we look at examples of three kinds of collaboration:

- Students collaborating with each other
- Teachers collaborating with their students
- Teachers collaborating with each other

Pulling the pieces apart in this way allows us to look closely at different instances of collaboration and figure out how each one works. However, to some extent, the distinctions are artificial. Teachers are always in the mix, even when students are teaming up with their peers. It's the teacher who puts the collaboration in motion by modeling and talking through all the parameters. It's the teacher who figures out the logistics of teaming, often in classes of 35 or more students. And it's the teacher who works productively with other colleagues to explore best practices and new ideas. The examples and stories that follow demonstrate what collaborating can do for learning and motivation, and how to create collaborative events that are most likely to succeed.

CAPTURING THE BIG IDEA OF COLLABORATION

Real-World Writing: Collaboration Is the Name of the Game

In the world outside the classroom, writing gets done by collaborating. In 1988 Stephen Witte, a man who was ahead of his time, investigated how workers collaborated to produce writing products, sometimes by working in committees, or editing each other's work, or writing one part of a larger piece, or incorporating/referring to each other's report writing in their letters and memos. "Even writers physically isolated in their garrets from others never really worked alone, and no text in the seven contexts I studied was ever created *ex nihilo* [out of nothing]" (Witte, 1988, p. 10).

Fast forward to this century in Silicon Valley, often considered "the most competitive, dog-eat-dog, I-will-sue-you-if-you-even-think-about-infringing-my-patents innovation hub in the world."

"Sure competition here is sharp-elbowed," said Reid Hoffman, a co-founder of LinkedIn. "But no one can succeed by themselves. Apple today is totally focused on how it can better work with its [applications] developer community." It cannot thrive without them. "The only way you can achieve something magnificent is by working with other people," said Hoffman (Friedman, 2013, paras. 3 and 8).

In the film and television industry, collaborative scriptwriting can translate to fame and fortune:

> What do feature films like *Annie Hall, The People vs. Larry Flynt, Batman Forever, Shrek, Election, Good Will Hunting, America's Sweetheart, There's Something About Mary,* and *O Brother, Where Art Thou?* have in common besides their success?. . . They were co-written by collaborative screen writing teams. (Johnson & Stevens, 2002, p. 1)

Screenwriters face a cold world, regardless of whether they write alone or in partnership. "The misery curve for screenwriters is legendary," according to Johnson and Stevens (2002), who interviewed 20 script teams to find out how and why they collaborate. "It's a daunting task to write a screenplay and even more daunting to write a good one" (p. 3). Bottom line: Sharing the writing is the way to go for all kinds of reasons. Two imaginations are better than one. It takes at least two to brainstorm. Working together improves motivation, work habits, even mental health. "Your partner can spark you and push you forward," says screenwriter Larry Karaszewski (p. 17). And if that isn't enough, working together makes for better writing. As Johnson and Stevens explain, "your writing partner can be an invaluable critic—your first audience. His or her response produces a better script than you could have come up with alone" (p. 20).

Research Favors Collaborative Learning

It's no surprise that research over the years consistently shows collaborating and working in teams is a big asset when it comes to learning. After analyzing a decade of studies on collaboration, researcher Susan Williams (2009) reports that "students working in collaborative groups learn more than those in traditional classrooms. . . . whether the task is simple or complex, collaborative learning results in moderate but significant gains in academic achievement in comparison to traditional learning" (p. 12). More specifically for writing, in a meta-analysis of research on writing instruction, Graham & Perin (2007) found that "collaborative arrangements in which students help each other with one or more aspects of their writing have a strong positive impact on quality" (p. 16).

But our new favorite study is the one showing that brain capacity builds when people work together. (We have a whole new neural highway system in place after coauthoring this book.) Now here's research that's worth spreading around:

> In a new study called, "How Social Interaction and Teamwork Led to Human Intelligence" posted in the Proceedings of the Royal Society B (1), researchers discovered that . . . the development of the human intellect is actually improved by being a team player. They found that teamwork requires people to navigate and build a complex network of relationships.
>
> This means that effective cooperation is both rewarding for the individual as well as the group as a whole. Cooperation actually makes us smarter! (Van Edwards, 2012, paras. 2–3)

It goes without saying that our students already know a lot about collaboration. In the social networking world where they operate every day, collaboration is in the drinking water. Fingers fly; responses appear instantly; everything is public, sometimes painfully so. By definition, writers depend on their audiences to keep the enterprise meaningful and moving along. Why not take advantage of this?

TAKING THE PLUNGE:
TEACHING STUDENTS TO COLLABORATE

Peer Response Groups

> The secret to successful peer response is a whole lot of teaching.

When the California Writing Project was in its infancy, Miles Myers (1982) conducted a survey of teachers by way of each site's summer institutes. Participants reported the kinds of practices they used in their classrooms. In addition, they looked at pieces of student writing and used these as a basis for devising lessons that also revealed their preferred teaching strategies. It turned out that institute teachers tended to avoid the risky business of peer response groups.

We can speculate on the reasons. Classroom chaos. Students off task. Teachers rushing from group to group. And there's more. Bad memories: Barbara Buckley, a long-time high school teacher in Danville, California, long harbored a grudge against collaboration that somehow fails to be collaborative:

> I have always hated group work. As a kid, I always ended up doing the bulk of the work and being bossy. As a teacher, I watched a repeat of my childhood experience every time my students were in groups. Then, about 20 years ago, my principal said that one of the main reasons people get fired from jobs is not incompetence, but rather inability to work and collaborate with others. For some reason, that idea rang true for me. I decided the problem with group work is that kids need to be taught how to collaborate. I learned to structure group assignments with explicit directions, procedures, and outcomes. (personal communication, April 9, 2014)

Nancy Atwell (1987) addresses the need for "explicit directions, procedures, and outcomes" by conducting procedural minilessons, including modeling and describing, throughout the school year. For Atwell, group-work often takes the form of peer conferences:

> I'll ask a writer to join me at the front of the room and read a piece of writing aloud for my response. I'll model appropriate response first, looking at the writer's face, listening, paraphrasing, then asking just a couple of questions about something I'd like to know more about. When I'm finished, I ask the rest of the class to describe what they saw me doing. The next day I'll model a truly awful response to the same piece of writing. This time, as the writer reads, I make all the mistakes I made as a novice responder and all the kinds of remarks kids make when they're not helping each other with their writing. I look at the piece

of writing instead of the writer, or I look around the room. As soon as the writer finishes reading I jump in with a story about a similar experience of my own. I make judgments: "Well, that was boring," or "Great. Really great. Really, really great. Really."(p. 129)

Atwell returns to the minilessons as many times as necessary, whenever she listens in on student conferences and hears them going astray. And repetition is one of the tickets to making collaboration work.

In Chapter 2 we offered some ideas for setting up peer response groups. The setup, however, is not a one-time event. It happens in some form over and over again in order to reinforce what it means to invest in someone else's writing, to scaffold increasingly sophisticated responses, and to tailor responses to different kinds of writing or writing situations.

Learning what to say about a peer's draft takes practice and lots of modeling. Moffett (1981) concentrates on a handful of specific, useful comments for students to make:

1. *Describe* what the piece seems like so far and the impressions you had about various points as you read or heard it. . . .
2. *Ask* the author questions that occur to you. . . .
3. Let the *author ask* questions about what he wants responses to. . . .
4. Take a *what-if approach.* Help the author test out what he's got so far by seeing what difference it would make if you changed this or that—added or deleted something, reordered some things, shifted emphasis, and so on. . . .
5. *Make up a title* for the piece under consideration . . . responders each make up a title after reading or hearing the draft, write it on a slip, and reveal these one at a time. . . . (pp. 22–23)

Whether or not these are the right types of comment for every circumstance, they offer some advantages for students in the learning stages. They steer away from critical judgments. They reveal to the writer if the piece has hit the mark, especially if the writer hears the reader give an impression or interpretation far from what he or she expected. Writers also benefit from hearing the titles proposed by their peers, as these are signs of unity and intention. Wide variations may give the writer a hint about where to shore things up.

For teachers and students with access to technology, programs like Google Docs enable collaborative writing and responding in ways Moffett never imagined. Students can compose and revise in "real time" and in a more real-world way. Teacher comments can be part of the process when those comments will do the most good. And because so many adult writers use collaborative writing tools in business and other professional settings, students can practice what is, for now, the way writing often happens outside the classroom.

DIVING DEEPER:
TEACHING STUDENTS TO COLLABORATE ONLINE

Collaboration adds zing to projects and assignments and gives students extra stamina to see them through long-term, challenging work.

As wonderful as it is when students have some kind of equipment either at home or at school so they can work together, they still need to learn the etiquette for collaboration, how to be collegial and thoughtful and downright helpful. In fact, the need for teaching on all fronts may be even greater when technology is involved. Teachers like Liz Harrington who have made the transition to online collaboration have gone one step at a time, testing the water before going off the high dive.

Case Study: Book Club Blogs

Middle school teacher Liz Harrington is a long-time proponent of independent reading and student book clubs. Over the years she has built a sizeable classroom library and a practice of talking about books among students who bring multiple perspectives and cultural backgrounds to the conversation. The only problem: time. The book clubs were eating up too much of it. So she decided to try something new.

She introduced the idea of book club blogs to one class first just to see how things would go, and she kept the guidelines simple (see Figure 5.1).

Now, with years of book blog experience under her belt, Harrington knows what to expect: "In September, the blogs are mostly summary," says Harrington. "That's where my teaching begins. I bring in student models from previous years and I also model how to write a brief summary." Harrington teaches students how to write specifically about "why they like what they like," how to pull out specific examples from the text, and how to comment on those examples. And she makes the most of the built-in audience: "I tell the students it's important they write blogs that someone would want to read." Because Harrington uses the blogs as scaffolding for teaching students to write literary analysis at a later time, these lessons about audience, specificity, and analysis set the stage. (All Harrington quotes, including Figures 5.1 and 5.2, are from a personal communication, April 18, 2014.) When it comes to writing constructive responses to the book club blogs, Harrington again provides guidelines and models for her students (see Figure 5.2).

During the course of the year, Harrington notes that the students' writing changes as a result of peer and teacher comments in addition to lessons and modeling. "The students up their game a little bit. They take each other's comments and build on them. And of course, a lot of learning comes from seeing how others write a blog post."

Figure 5.1. Guidelines for Book Club Blogs

1. You will be responsible for posting to your own blog at http://kidblog.org at least once every 2 weeks.
2. In addition, you will be responsible for commenting on the blogs of each member of your book club, at least once every 2 weeks.
3. Your blog post will focus on the book you are currently reading. It should include the following information:
   - Title and author.
   - Page you are currently on.
   - The plot so far (try to avoid "spoilers"): This should be very brief—3 or 4 sentences at most.
   - Your commentary on the book so far: This should be the longest and most detailed part of your blog post.
     » What do you like, and why?
     » What, if anything, do you dislike, and why?
   - A quote from this week's reading that seems important or memorable to you.
   - Commentary on the quote, showing why you think it is important or memorable. **Commentary should be specific and detailed.**
   - Anything else you would like to share about your book.
4. Each blog post will receive up to 20 homework points, based on completion and the depth of thought reflected in the post.
5. All blog posts will be screened before final posting. If your post is taken down, you will have to revise and repost it.

Figure 5.2. Guidelines for Commenting on Blogs

1. Use polite and academic language in your comments.
2. Comment on what the writer **wrote**, not on the writer himself/herself.
3. Be **specific** in your comments. Don't say, "Your post was really good." Instead, refer to something specific that you like about it.
4. Don't focus on things like grammar and spelling. Focus on ideas instead.
5. Don't put the writer down, even in a joking way. Humor does not always come across effectively in blog comments.
6. Don't use your comments as an opportunity to show how much smarter you are than the writer of the blog.
7. Use academic language, and follow the rules of grammar and spelling as much as possible. In particular, be sure to capitalize correctly and avoid unnecessary abbreviations. This is a scholarly blog, not a social one.
8. Avoid the use of "all caps." It may lead to the reader misunderstanding your tone.
9. Comments will receive points according to how complete they are, and how well these guidelines have been followed.
10. Before submitting a comment, always consider whether you would be happy to read that same comment on your work.

Harrington describes the book club blogs as "part of the DNA of the classroom." If anything, the culture of talking about books that prompted Herrington to establish book clubs in the first place is enhanced. "There's lots more informal talk about reading. Kids recommend and exchange books. Even parents read the blogs." And there's a spin-off that no one anticipated. The blogs give students a chance to connect culturally and cross-culturally. "I had a Vietnamese student who was particularly attracted to a book set in Vietnam. She recommended it on this basis. Another Vietnamese student learned about the book from her blog and immediately decided to read it."

It's worth noting how Harrington meets the challenge of teaching students to collaborate. Her approach is a graceful mix of academic and social lessons: on one hand, how to quote from a book and on the other, how to comment respectfully. At the same time, Harrington instills the idea that writing and talking about reading is something literate people do.

Seventh-Grade Student Writings. This book blog and these responses are spring term efforts after students have benefited from months of instruction and practice. The blog writer goes beyond simple summary to include specific examples and relevant commentary. The responders tailor their remarks, focusing on ideas rather than wandering into less useful territory.

The Avengers

By Britney Gallego

March 20, 2014 @ 7:15 PM 5 COMMENTS

I just finished reading *The Avengers* by Joss Whedon. This book was about the Marvel movie that came to theaters in 2012. This book/movie is about Captain America, Iron Man, Thor, Hulk, Black Widow, and Hawkeye. These super-heroes have to battle Loki, Thor's adopted brother. Loki's plan was to take over the Earth and rule it because he couldn't rule Asgard (Thor's planet/Realm). In the end this group of heroes will battle and try to win back the Earth and defeat Loki.

One thing I liked about this amazing book is the sensory details the author adds to this book. I really enjoy books that have sensory details because it helps me visualize the characters and places told in the story. An important example of this is when Joss Whedon states, "He opened a secure box. Inside was illuminated red circuitry . . . an unusual glittering blue cube.

. . .

It crackled with electricity, and forks of charged current danced around it" (127). This quote shows the features of the Tesseract and how much power it could generate. In addition, this quote helped me visualize the most powerful weapon in this story. Overall, this story is very good due to the sensory details.

Since there wasn't anything I disliked about this book, another thing I did like was the sense of humor the author added to almost every chapter in this story and movie. An example of this in the story is when Iron Man states, "'I've been in captivity for three months, there are a few things I want. Two. One, I want an American cheeseburger, and the other is I want you to call for a press conference now.'" (48). This quote shows that even though Tony Stark just got rescued from being in captivity he refuses to go to the doctor. Also this quote shows that a hamburger from California is the main thing Tony needed once he got back to the United States.

All in all, this was a very good book to read due to the reasons I have mentioned. This book and the movie both have a lot of action and the book has wonderful sensory details which is why I really enjoy reading and watching *The Avengers* by Joss Whedon.

Comments on Britney's Blog

By Raymond Lo

March 25, 2014 at 8:08 PM

Britney, your blog was very interesting. First, your first paragraph is great because your introduction provided background information and other facts that we needed to know to understand your blog. Your last sentence ends with a twist. I wish I could write better twists as my last sentence of my paragraph. Your second paragraph is great because you describe the excellent sensory details that the author presents in the book. I especially liked your description of the author's great sensory details. This quote shows the features of the Tesseract and how much power it could generate. In addition, this quote helped me visualize the most powerful weapon in this story. This commentary showed me that Whedon was indeed a good author for this kind of book and set for the hero and villain genre. Your third paragraph tells me what a excellent book that you described because from your point of view this book has no flaws. You also make this book sound like the best book in the world. I wish I could make books sound like that. I like your choice of quotes it is funny. Your rating is awesome because it is reasonable and logical because I watched the movie.

Comments on Britney's Blog

By Edward Tran

March 25, 2014 at 8:55 PM

Britney, this sounds like a interesting book. I really like how you kept your summary short and detailed without giving out spoilers. I also really like how you clarified things using parentheses to make it make more sense. I really like your organization, how you separated the two reasons you like the book. On the other hand, I think you should add more info what u like. For example, things that you like about the author or scenes that you really like. I really like how you add evidence to support your statement followed with commentary. Perhaps, you could add more. What also caught my eye was that you stated that you didn't dislike anything which show the reader you really love the book. I do agree that the quote shows lots of sensory detail. "He opened a secure box. Inside was illuminated red circuitry . . . an unusual glittering blue cube . . . It crackled with electricity, and forks of charged current danced around it." (127).

Thoughts on Audience, Collaboration, and Technology

It seems the student commenters have paid especially close attention to Britney's blog. No skimming the surface. Raymond Lo points to specific paragraphs, sentences, and quotations that enhance the writing and gives special attention to features of the blog that he wishes to emulate (e.g., endings with a twist). Edward Tran also comments on what works in the writing (e.g., organization, use of evidence) and makes several recommendations, albeit rather loose ones.

Harrington credits the regularity of the blog assignment for giving students "the familiarity and confidence to respond to the work of their peers." In addition, she notes, "For this purpose, I'm really trying to get students to comment on the thinking of the writer of the post, rather than on the quality of the writing." We might also observe that the students are in this together. They are at the same time, the blog poster and the commenter, the writer and the audience. To some extent, these dual roles may influence their comments.

In fact, when students comment on text and on others' comments about text, they are engaging in reflective thought or "critical thinking," according to Sheridan Blau (2010), Professor of English and Education Emeritus, University of California–Santa Barbara. What's more, Blau calls this kind of writing "the defining characteristic of college-level discourse" (p. 53).

Harrington's case also prompts several questions. First, what keeps students from bogging down when they have to write blogs over a whole year? "Having peers comment on and share their thoughts about what they are reading is a motivating factor," says Harrington. But there's another ingredient at work here. "Engaging with a text is a habit of mind," explains Harrington. "It's not something that is set apart for when we 'do' literary analysis."

Since Harrington switched from book clubs to book blogs, it's also fair to question whether technology buys any special benefits. Going digital is certainly not a panacea. But as it turns out, classroom activities that integrate technology with small reading groups (literature circles, book clubs) pay off in several ways, according to a recent review of research. Specifically, these activities have the potential to:

- Connect students to readers outside the classroom
- Provide written records of classroom discussion that can be analyzed by teachers and students
- Increase motivation and engagement
- Give voice to marginalized students
- Develop new literacies skills
- Foster classroom community and social interaction
- Meet individual needs by providing time to think
- Improve student learning (Coffey, 2012, p. 402)

One more plug for collaboration through technology. Some teachers have discovered that students write well when they actually write together. Anne Moege, an English teacher in a South Dakota middle school, used to have students write individual summaries of their reading in preparation for literature circles. When students tried the same activity, working collaboratively on wikis, "Moege found that digital tools allowed such writing to happen more efficiently and more powerfully than ever before" (National Writing Project, 2010, p. 45). Students still have to learn to write a summary, not to mention how to collaborate productively, but they have the benefit of learning from each other and bringing their combined insights to the task.

DIVING IN AGAIN:
TEACHING STUDENTS TO COLLABORATE ON LONG-TERM PROJECTS

The idea of project-based learning shows up prominently on the Internet, in books, and on the teacher radar, along with all the essentials like giving students choices and responsibilities, establishing question(s) to investigate, using technology, getting feedback, and making presentations. Our focus here is on what makes projects really tick. It's the teamwork, the very team work that students will encounter countless times in their lives—from personal pursuits like serving on volunteer committees to professional assignments as complex as building bridges or fighting diseases.

Case Study: Collaboration and Civic Engagement

When high school teacher Judy Kennedy proposed the idea of a civic action project to her three government classes, the 12th-graders were understandably puzzled. "We had studied inequities in income and opportunity, but of course, they couldn't yet imagine a role for themselves in making things better," says Kennedy.

The starting point, then, was to think about what makes an effective citizen. Students created lists together, eventually winnowing them down to the most important points—a list that could be revisited during the course of the project. Kennedy's goal was for her students to learn the *steps* to fix a problem—not to fix the problem itself. In the process, she wanted students to do something they cared deeply about and to do it with people who shared that passion. "The minute students got to choose their own groups —3 to 5 classmates—that was the ticket. I emphasized picking friends— people you text—because they had to do so much work outside of class."

Kennedy used the Constitutional Rights Foundation's Civic Action Project (CAP) website (www.crfcap.org) to guide the project. Students had to conduct five civic actions in connection with their chosen problem, for example, conducting research, interviews, surveys; attending board or community meetings; making posters; writing blog posts, letters, and emails; making people aware of a problem.

Students visited the computer lab once a week for 8 weeks, looking at websites Kennedy provided, but also learning to search on their own.

> The kids really worked together. They talked about different kinds of search words, tried to interpret what they were looking at, and shared everything they found. They delegated—"you look up this and I'll look up that." Kids really liked researching together and finding links. They are naturally curious and don't necessarily do this kind of thing every day. The computer lab was also a place where they could collaborate on setting up their surveys, writing interview questions, coming up with blogs, and taking notes. (All Kennedy quotes are from a personal communication, April 5, 2014.)

Kennedy notes that "kids were into it," but they also suffered from adolescent grand expectations. "They wanted to take a problem and go straight to the top. Let's not start with the vice principal. Let's go to the superintendent." Kennedy also cautions that students are disappointed when they don't get immediate responses to their letters or emails. "In their instant gratification way of thinking, they expected to hear right back."

But students did make significant connections with people in the school and community. For instance, they interviewed the school principal about topics like bullying and sex education. They turned to teachers they knew to ask how they handled homophobia in the classroom. One student interviewed a parent who was a probation officer about marijuana, and another student interviewed a parent who worked in an animal shelter about animal abuse.

Kennedy nudged and encouraged the students to seek out people who would pay attention. For instance, one set of students focused on an issue with the overcrowded county bus that left students behind on school mornings. Rather than try to talk to an administrator at the transit agency, Kennedy suggested that students interview the bus driver:

> Students first have to work up the courage to talk to adults in
> a respectful, intelligent manner about the problems they think
> need fixing. They need to learn to do the legwork, understand the
> underlying problem, and figure out the questions before they go to the
> CEO. My job is to teach them how to do their homework and how to
> follow the chain of command.

According to Kennedy, students genuinely cared about their projects. They picked topics that might never reach the "top ten list" if adults had been dreaming them up. For example, one team focused on the piles of pigeon poop that forced students to leave the sidewalk and take to the street when walking to school. Their goal was to alert city authorities and to convince them to clean it up. "Students never lost momentum," says Kennedy. "They loved working with friends on real problems of their choosing."

Kennedy tracked her students' progress in several ways. During their time in the computer lab, she interacted with all of the groups, moving from one to the next, helping them gather and make sense of information, commenting on credibility of sources. She also invited students to make appointments with her before and after school and during lunch. Each day that students worked on their projects in class, they turned in a short report about what they did, what websites they used, and what they learned. They stapled notes and printouts to these reports and kept them in their folders as a resource.

When it came to the final write-ups, students helped each other by swapping ideas and information, but in the end, they each wrote about their own journey: how they came to their topic, what happened along the way, what they learned, and what they would do differently. Then they shared what they wrote with three other people not on their teams. "It was an opportunity for students to teach each other what they learned. And kids were fascinated by the projects." Kennedy notes that for the purposes of a presentation, student teams can create videos, PowerPoints, and public service announcements.

Thoughts About Student Motivation and Real-World Projects

What sustains a project over a 2-month period, while other things are going on during class time and when so much of the project depends on out-of-class work? In this case, there is a dynamic duo at play: choice and collaboration. Students choose their issues and their collaborators; they decide on the steps, on who does what and on how they do it. And because the projects deal with realities outside the classroom, students are so absorbed that they don't wait for the finish line to tell everyone what they're finding as they go along. Kennedy says that phrases like "can you believe this?" float through the classroom when students make a new discovery. This isn't just civic engagement; it's full-on student engagement.

One proponent of setting up genuine situations—ones that call for real communication—was James Britton (1970), who cautioned against what he called "dummy runs." Rather, Britton believed that students need to talk, read, and write in school for functional purposes, in other words "to make sense of the world" rather than for some made-up exercise. Britton calls for students to take on literacy activities that "offer genuine challenge, and result in the extension and deepening of their experience" (p. 130).

Part of the package when it comes to long-term projects is the problem of motivation. Remember the script partners profiled earlier in this chapter? Their projects last for years. "Conventional wisdom says it takes five to ten years to learn the *craft* of screenwriting, and five to ten screen plays before you finally sell one," say Johnson and Stevens (2002, p. 3). In this exchange, script partners Lee and Janet Scott Batchler of *Batman Forever* fame explain that it's the collaboration that helps them stay motivated:

> *Janet:* Sometimes we both get down at the same time. It just works
>   that way. Sometimes we sort of pull each other through.
> *Lee:* The best baseball player in the world has a batting slump.
> *Janet:* And the best baseball players in the world are batting
>   somewhere in the .300s. Nobody hits a thousand. We just have to
>   keep reminding each other of that. We sort of have to goose each
>   other to get going sometimes. (Johnson & Stevens, 2002, p. 4)

In both the Harrington and Kennedy stories above, spurring each other on seems to be the bottom line. Students motivate students.

Student Writing. In their write-ups for Kennedy's class, students described how their choice of problems evolved. For example, Keenan Johnson explains how his group's interest in teen pregnancy took a particular direction:

> After doing research, we found that most of teen pregnancies were
> unplanned and/or accidents. We wondered why teen pregnancies are

happening accidentally when sex education is being taught to students. That's where we got the idea to find out what is being taught in these sex education classes and what is not being taught, but should be to give teens a heads up on different situations.

Student Kenneth Aguiluz, on the other hand, had a personal connection to his project on the rehabilitation of the Hayward shoreline. "I grew up going there, whether it was to go watch the birds, fish with my grandfather, walk there on the trail with my grandmother. There was so much history with it just in my life. I always thought it was a peaceful place to go and be in nature."

Students wrote about the kinds of things they learned from their research and interviews that informed their civic actions. Jessica Flores learned about things that motivate bullies:

Many bullies choose to pick on other kids because they are having problems at home. No one is showing them love and they come from families who are always angry or screaming. Bullies pick on others because they've been bullied before or because they want to feel big and powerful.

Another member of the group concerned with bullies, Ifeoma Udemezue, details one of their civic actions:

We took advantage of special events in school and in the community to increase people's awareness about our project. We even used events as an opportunity to engage people in discussion and pass on information in person. For example, I am a member of YAC (Youth Advisory Council) which serves as a bridge between the youth community and the City Council by making suggestions and providing feedback regarding issues affecting and concerning the youth of San Leandro. As a member we are required to attend every city council meeting. I took advantage of the opportunity to pitch a policy to the council members concerning bullying awareness. Initially, my policy was to make sure students in San Leandro elementary schools be required to be schooled on why bullying is harmful and why it is so important to tell someone if you are being picked on. This was a huge proposal and although we didn't quite achieve our goal with making this a policy, we got people thinking which is what really counts. And I believe before shaping the world you must shape your community.

The write-ups were filled with reflections about what students learned about being effective citizens. In addition to learning a whole lot about animal cruelty and neglect, Josephine Luna grew as a compassionate citizen:

Some skills that I gained after this experience were open-mindedness; I now know not everyone is going to feel the same way as I do. I also learned how to communicate well with others, and how to be more professional with the things I say or do. I also gained a voice; I know now that I'm not the only one who wants to be heard. There are many people who want change just as bad as I do. My attitude changed dramatically throughout this experience. At first I thought that no one really cares and no one was going to give us the time of day, but now I know that I was completely wrong. People do actually care, and do want to hear what we have to say. By doing little things like these civic actions, I do believe that it is possible to make change in our society.

Not everything was sunshine and roses for the students. Taylar Keene commented on a common problem when students—in this case, one of her group members—are trying to conduct online research at school.

Cheyenne wrote an email to the district, expressing her opinion about how the district has a lock on the word "sex" when you want to search something on Google. How can they possibly expect us to learn about having safe sex and they don't even let us search it? Cheyenne was trying to get them to understand that we are not young children anymore and with growing up in a world that moves as fast as it does now, we need all the help and advice we can get on any subject, especially this one.

Thoughts About Managing Long-Term Projects

Projects like Kennedy's incorporate many of the big ideas in the CCSS, in addition to using technology for the purposes of producing writing and collaborating with others. Students also conduct research, gather evidence, draft and revise for specific purposes and audiences, and traverse a spectrum of argumentative and informational writing—all this without sacrificing student enjoyment!

As exciting as projects like Kennedy's can be for students, there's a need for management tools and strategies to keep the lid from blowing off. At the outset of the project when students start to fret, Kennedy invites them to write down their questions. From these, she puts together an FAQ sheet—shown in Figure 5.3—something students can hang on to for the duration. (Some of the information in the FAQ, for example, the list of civic actions in question 3, show up in various places on the ever-evolving CAP website: www.crfcap.org/mod/page/view.php?id=82.)

Figure 5.3. Guidelines for A Civic Action Project

Civic Action Project—Frequently Asked Questions

1. What exactly are we doing?

    Answer: You are choosing a real problem, issue, or policy that you are concerned about that you want to see changed in the community. You are learning the steps to take to fix the problem.

2. Why are we doing this?

    Answer: You learn best by doing. By examining a real problem, you can better learn how government works. You can also gain the skills and confidence to participate and gain the understanding of how your civic actions can make a difference.

3. What is a civic action? How many do we have to do?

    Answer: You will do five of any combination of the actions below. Civic actions are:

    • Finding out more about a problem—reading articles, talking to people, finding out who or what agencies share your concerns, doing surveys.

    • Developing your strategy for addressing the problem—determining what your goal is, what do you think should happen. Deciding what you need and who to ask.

    • Contacting people/agencies that could address the situation—calling, writing, emailing, visiting people who might be able to solve the problem.

    • Making other persons aware of your concerns—talking to people to get them to support your position, creating a poster or flier campaign to raise awareness, using the Internet (blog, web page, and so on).

    • Becoming involved in the efforts of others to address the problem.

    • Trying to get the problem on the agendas of different groups (bring the problem to the attention of school leaders, neighborhood councils, city council, school board). Or bring the problem to the appropriate agency like the Better Business Bureau, Chamber of Commerce, Department of Housing, or to an advocacy group. Remember that doing the research to find out what agencies and groups might help you is a civic action.

    • Taking political action—lobbying, petitioning, testifying at hearings and other public meetings, working to get something on the ballot, voting, and so on. (Constitutional Rights Foundation, n.d.)

4. Are we working in groups or individually?

    Answer: It is your choice. You can work individually, in pairs, or with two other people (no more than five to a group).

5. When are we starting this?

    Answer: You need to fill out the Civic Action Proposal and give it to me by Wednesday, 11/20.

6. When will the project end?

    Answer: At the end of the semester.

7. How many points is this project worth?

    Answer: It will be the majority of your second-quarter points.

8. Is there a guide or rubric for this project?

    Answer: Yes. I will show it to you and remind you of it along the way.

This kind of assignment sheet accounts for the nitty gritty, like deadlines and points, but it also lets students know what they are supposed to learn. Because it is born from the students' own questions, it may carry a different kind of weight and authenticity than an assignment that is strictly teacher -generated. And no doubt about it, students need written information to keep them on task over the long haul. The civic engagement project is only one of their many obligations—academic and social—so something like an FAQ is a handy reference.

Another highly recommended management tool is a tracking sheet to be filled out daily or weekly by individuals or teams. It might look something like the one in Figure 5.4.

Figure 5.4. A Management Tool for Long-Term Projects

Tracking Sheet

Name: _____ Name of Project Team: _____

Work accomplished today: _____

Collaborators: _____

Next steps: _____

Problems or concerns: _____

Sign up to consult with teacher or others in class (include names): _____

_____

Submit this form electronically at the end of each class period to the teacher and to anyone with whom you wish to consult.

One of the big advantages of a tracking sheet is that it puts the ball in the right court. Students are responsible for organizing their work and their time. Especially when a project spans several weeks or months, a tracking sheet does just what it says: It keeps track of all the pieces for both students and teachers. Tracking sheets can be simple or detailed, depending on the project and also on the extent to which students need help with study skills.

Sometimes it makes sense to identify a project manager for each group or to rotate the managing role among group members. Student managers can help to keep the enterprise going, even when the going gets rough, without the teacher having to intervene every time. It's all the better when these roles happen naturally, growing out of individual strengths and the needs of the group. But designating managers has the advantage of spreading the wealth and building leadership skills.

Here are some other classroom-tested ideas for establishing outcomes, keeping students on task, and creating momentum:

- Establish a timeline.
- Set firm deadlines.
- Assign roles and responsibilities.
- Make each individual accountable. (See tracking sheet in Figure 5.4.)
- Develop routines for collaborating.
- Solicit help from your school's technology person, if available, or from other faculty who may have community contacts, and from parents/community members who might bring in special expertise.
- Set a minimum amount of expected time for students to work on the project outside of class.

One thing that is not easily managed is online accessibility at school to controversial topics. As Kennedy's student, Taylor Keene, complained, "How can they [the district] possibly expect us to learn about having safe sex and they don't even let us search it?" It is possible in some districts to ask for a waiver for particular websites or topics. But as we all know, students can find out what they want to know right on their smartphones or on other equipment outside of school.

TEACHERS COLLABORATING WITH STUDENTS

Developing a Community of Writers

> In a collaborative classroom, all members share what they know. In the case of writing, this sharing makes a complex task more approachable, more open to possibilities, and more doable.

Sometimes it happens in the middle of an ordinary day during an ordinary lesson. Without warning, students and teacher take off together to an unplanned destination. High school teacher Sue Threatt, for one, never expected to hook up with her students around a job usually reserved for teachers alone:

> After returning some papers to an 11th-grade U.S. History class, I offered the usual opportunity for questions. Many of the students were especially critical of the assignment wording. After some discussion, Sophia, a predictably outspoken contributor to any classroom discussion, quipped about teacher language and suggested that students could "translate" teacher instructions or at least add additional explanations. From that day on, I invited student feedback

about assignment instructions *before* the assignment was given and *while* the assignment unfolded. Not only did I learn more about how to construct classroom work and life, but students learned more about their own writing, its purposes, and why teachers do what they do. It was an inclusive, theory-validating thing to do. We all learned about human communication and how working together can be real and educative for everyone involved. (personal communication, March 19, 2014)

There's a lot of talk these days about engaging students, as if the teacher has to conjure up ways to keep them interested and entertained. What happens here, however, is that Sophia is not afraid to speak up, and in turn, her teacher is not afraid to jump on a new idea that ultimately gives her students a bona fide role in setting the agenda for their writing. Collaboration in this case means mutual investment, and you can't do much better than that.

However, we do not want to minimize the effort it takes to bring students in on the action. We are reminded of another teacher who became understandably frazzled by the give-and-take with her students. At one point she threw her arms up and shouted, "What do you think this is—a democracy?"

We vote for collaborations that happen because two or more people are excited about the same thing, like the one that took place in a garage when the two Steves—Jobs and Wozniak—invented the original Apple computer. There are countless stories in the modern world of people putting their heads together around a common interest or problem:

> For example, in early 2003 the SARS virus spread rapidly until it was realized that it had become a global crisis. At this point 11 laboratories in 9 countries collaborated to control its spread. Connected by a network and shared website as well as constant emails and teleconferences, the labs shared data in real-time and within one month this collaboration had identified the pathogen and sequenced its DNA. (Williams, 2009, p. 5)

We can imagine that these scientists stayed on task. No one threw paper wads or texted friends or applied mascara. But looking past the fact that they behaved like adults, we spot the secret ingredient: They cared about the same thing.

A classroom community of writers has some similarities to the global SARS team besides a shared interest. Its members are more or less on equal footing even though more experienced participants may have a little more clout. People share what they know and help each other. They ask and give advice. No one holds back. It's all for one and one for all.

And of course, there are differences. A community of writers is not pressed to the wall to solve a life-and-death problem. It can evolve gently. In fact, it doesn't even have a starting gate or a finish line. It grows in pace with its members, every one of whom is a writer. And it flourishes when teacher and students alike share their writing and their writing lives with each other.

Author Andrea W. Herrmann laments that she never let her students in on what she learned as a writer: her aches and pains with writer's block and using a computer; the writers she turned to for ideas and inspiration; quick, incidental conversations with her husband that spurred her on. For students, the very notion that writers do not simply pour words onto the page is a comfort and, in the case of Herrmann (1991), a source of amusement:

> Of course, I have never admitted my own eating/writing disorder to anyone; even my husband doesn't know. Normally I am a sensible, low fat, high fruits and vegetables, eater. That is, when the writing goes well. When blocked, the culinary rules change. For example, today since 9:30 A.M., when I began struggling to write this essay, I have eaten six large chocolate chip cookies (defrosted in batches of two in the microwave), one heavily salted hardboiled egg, and three slices of toast smothered in strawberry jam. I have drunk several cups of herbal tea, including a cup of sweetened ginseng—for memory and energy—and a cup of hot chocolate.
>
> By 1:51 P.M. I have eaten the cupboard bare and now must take a shopping break to lay in supplies for the remainder of my writing day. I will buy "finger food" that permits me to eat with one hand and keyboard with the other. (p. 180)

Aside from sharing writing processes—where ideas come from (in the shower?), what kind of rituals you observe (walking around aimlessly, dusting off tabletops, making coffee?), and how you tackle revision—writing community members think aloud with each other about what makes a good story, how to get started, how to hook a reader, how to make a graceful exit, where to put in dialogue, what kinds of details to include, how to know if the paper sings. And everyone writes together, both teacher and students.

Talking about everyone's writing processes and decisions opens up so many options for students, far more options than they would ever stumble on if left to their own devices. The same is true when teachers and students collaborate on the qualities of good writing. Students learn about qualities that are not just imitations of what one person—the teacher—values. At the same time, students can test out what they know about writing.

Case Study: Giving Students a Say-So in Evaluating Writing

Carl Whithaus (2005), Professor and Director of the University of California–Davis Writing Program, asks students what they think counts as successful writing:

After telling the students a little about myself and asking them to tell me their names and something memorable about themselves, I begin class by asking them to write down the criteria they consider important for good writing. I do not tell them what type of writing: I do not say academic or fiction; I simply ask them to write for a few minutes from their experience and explain to me what makes a piece of writing good. (pp. 51–52)

Whithaus goes on to explain: "I was determined to ask students about what they wanted to write and about how we should evaluate that writing. I needed to know how they saw writing and communicating in terms of their own needs." Whithaus's students wrote and read aloud things like "A good piece of writing is concise. . . . Writing is good when it gets the imagination going, when it makes you think. . . .Good writing uses correct English" (p. 53).

At the point when students began to lose interest—"their attention was drifting to the windows, the hallway, away from the reader's words"— Whithaus helped them pull the list of criteria together:

I said, "So we've got different definitions of good writing. Let's see if we can write some of these down and come to some sort of agreement. I heard 'concise.'" I wrote "concise" on the board. I was trying to back load my comments here; I wanted student discourse, the students' own words to serve as the basis for our evaluative criteria. Later in the semester, I often moved away from the front of the room during these types of activities, handing the chalk to students so that they can write on the board. (p. 53)

The payoff here is that Whithaus learns what his students know and he works from this foundation. At the same time, students get a stake in the process. It's not all about what the teacher thinks. It's about contributions. It's about battling it out together.

Some other areas for teacher–student collaboration are goal setting, selecting writing topics, deciding on procedures, creating rubrics, and any kind of debriefing. Suffice it to say if there were ever a discipline or endeavor where working together is profitable, it's writing.

TEACHERS COLLABORATING WITH EACH OTHER

The CCSS leave the teaching in the hands of teachers, where it absolutely should be. That doesn't mean, however, that teachers have to figure everything out by themselves. The idea of teachers teaching teachers is not a new one. For James Gray (2000), it popped up early in his career:

Shortly after I arrived at San Leandro in the fall of 1953, I was invited to share an experience that greatly affected my understanding of the power of collective teacher knowledge. A number of my colleagues in the San Leandro English department invited me to join them at the Asilomar conference in Pacific Grove, around the bay from Carmel. ... I signed up for the group on composition. The leader, whose role was to keep discussion moving and lively, was Barney Tanner, an English teacher from Palo Alto. The rest of us were also classroom teachers, experienced and inexperienced. For three days I listened to excited and clearly committed English teachers share their ideas and practices, their successes and questions and concerns. Which works of literature generate fresh student thinking and writing? What do we do when a student misinterprets a text but writes well? On the drive back to San Leandro, I very happily talked through my notes from the weekend and announced, "I have eighteen new ideas about teaching writing, and all of the ideas came from other classroom teachers!" (pp. 20–21)

> Those [teachers] who have access to teacher networks, enriched professional roles, and collegial work feel more efficacious in gaining the knowledge they need to meet the needs of their students and more positive about staying in the profession. (Darling-Hammond, 1996, p. 4)

For Gray, the seeds of the National Writing Project were planted early on by experiences like this one. NWP is now middle-aged, with 40 years of teachers' collective wisdom rippling broadly through the profession. Whether or not teachers participate in a project like this one, they certainly may want to join forces whenever they have the chance. The featured teachers in the following case studies happen to be Writing Project teachers, but they are also teachers who embrace the principles of teacher leadership and professionalism in other settings.

> "Teachers must be the primary driving force behind change. They are best positioned to understand the problems that students face and to generate possible solutions." James Stigler and James Hiebert (1999, p. 135).

Case Study: Collaborating on Lesson Design

It is an all too familiar scene: Teachers subjected to hours of deadly lectures about the Common Core State Standards. Imagine how many papers are graded, how many text messages are sent, how many to-do lists are created over the course of this "professional" development. Fortunately, some teachers have a different experience, investigating firsthand how the standards play out in the classroom.

Stan Pesick, former history teacher and currently Co-Director of the Oakland Unified School District/Mills College History/ELA Collaborative, works with 50 teachers of grades 6–12 to engage in conversations about argumentative writing. In small groups of three to four, the teachers construct a series of lessons on a particular moment in history, one of which they later try out in the classroom. This vehicle for collaboration, called "lesson study," offers great advantages for teachers, according to Pesick. "Rather than inviting in an outside person, teachers drive their own professional development. What's more, developing a lesson together makes it 'our' lesson. It's a democratic process" (personal communication, March 18, 2014).

The initial step is for teachers to develop both a student and a teacher question. The student question guides what goes into the lesson. The teacher question guides the investigation itself and addresses its overall purpose: What can we learn about the teaching and learning of argumentative writing? Here are examples of student/teacher questions from the lesson study groups:

Student question—Is John Brown an American hero?
Teacher question—How can guided annotation of historical
  documents help students develop a claim and write a paragraph
  that uses the annotations to explain evidence in support of the
  claim?

Student question—Was the Boston Massacre an act of self-defense or
  murder?
Teacher question—If we teach students explicit criteria for developing
  a strong thesis statement, will they use that criteria to develop their
  own thesis? (S. Pesick, personal communication, April 14, 2014)

Student question —How successful was the Populist Party?
Teacher question—How can we teach students to use evidence to
  support their argument? (Pesick, 2005, p. 3)

With "our" lesson in hand, one teacher in the group teaches while the rest watch. Later the group members meet and talk and look at student work to determine what worked and what didn't. Then they revise and teach the lesson again in a second classroom, after which they collect student writing and compare the refined lesson with the first one.

Pesick (2005) notes what it takes to make a lesson study successful:

Ultimately, lesson study should focus attention on teaching and learning, what was done and how did students respond, not on the teacher per se. So that in the debriefing, after a lesson is observed, group members will discuss how "our" lesson worked, not whether the teacher did a good job or not. (p. 4)

In the end, teachers write up an analysis: what they did, why they did it, what they learned, and next steps. They apply what they learned to other lessons, all of which they ultimately share with other teachers at department meetings and at conferences.

Pesick calls this lesson study project "an uncommon approach to the Common Core because history leads the way, rather than being an after-thought as it appears in the CCSS" (personal communication, March 18, 2014). He continues with these thoughts on the subject of history:

> Argumentative writing is at the center of the discipline. Historians make claims, use evidence and tease out reasons. Teaching argument is teaching disciplinary thinking. Another big bonus is that history engages students in questions with broad ethical issues. Kids gravitate to those kinds of questions.

Collaborating on a Dynamic Curriculum

Veteran teacher Pauline Sahakian (2001) experienced the satisfaction of designing a curriculum with a small group of teachers at a high school in Clovis, California. For many years, Sahakian and her colleagues had dreamed about "what we would do if we were in charge of the educational world" (p. 52). When their chance came, the teachers happily took a week in August to work together on a plan. One of the best things that happens in teaching is to sit down with other teachers to talk about what they want for their students and to hammer out a plan, to try out ideas on each other, to write and reflect, and along the way to laugh and enjoy each other. As Darling-Hammond says, "[Teachers who are able to collaborate with other teachers] are really engaged in it—in work where they are rolling up their sleeves to design and evaluate curriculum and instruction together in a way that allows them to share their expertise deeply and in a sustained and on-going fashion" (quoted by Collier, 2011, p. 12).

But the headiness of inventing and innovating comes with a caution. Sahakian (2001) describes "the inevitable death" of the once-heralded cur-riculum 8 years after its inception. As the school grew with new teachers, the curriculum lost its luster. The original band of teachers clung to what they had worked so hard to create to the exclusion of their recently arrived colleagues. Borrowing an apt metaphor from the school reform literature, Sahakian says, "We explorers had become settlers" (p. 57–58).

Indeed, a curriculum—if it is to be relevant—has to be open to questioning and responsive to new circumstances and to an ever-changing student population. Sahakian, now director of the University of California–Merced Writing Project, characterizes as stagnant a program that was once a source of tremendous pride. Were she to write the sequel to her story, she might note that curriculum in the era of scripts and pacing guides was even more carved in stone—one curriculum for the multitudes and for all time.

What follows are stories of teachers who share Sahakian's wisdom. Developing curriculum is like painting the Golden Gate Bridge: Once you get to the other end, you need to start all over again. The job is never done. It isn't enough for teachers to have only one opportunity in 1 year or in 5 years or in 10 years to share their knowledge, refine their goals, and create new ways to engage students in important learning activities.

Because matters of curriculum—indeed, all teaching decisions—have too often been assigned to those who are not in the classroom, we want to urge our colleagues to stay in charge. As added encouragement, we believe this could be the best season in a long time for teachers to collaborate with their colleagues on curriculum and successful teaching strategies. According to Linda Darling-Hammond, the "[Common Core standards may give teacher communities] something to plan around in a much more thoughtful way than many kinds of curricula in the past, which have been dominated by textbooks rather than a conception of learning and how it progresses" (quoted by Collier, 2011, p. 14).

In the case that follows, teachers collaborate on a dynamic curriculum, one that is revisited each summer in an effort to prepare students for college-level reading and writing.

Case Study: Transition to College (T2C)

Closing the gap. Giving underrepresented, underachieving students the right stuff for college. The problem has been around for decades. Simplistic solutions like canned programs or teacher-proof materials miss the mark entirely. As the term *teacher-proof* suggests, the goal is to minimize the teacher's flexibility to adapt the curriculum and, in its place, to insert a fixed curriculum package. At the other end of the spectrum, the idea that each individual high school teacher should figure out how to jumpstart a college prep curriculum that closes the gap is also purely magical thinking. This is a problem that calls for all hands on deck.

That's how it was in 1988 when Laura Stokes, then Director of the Area 3 Writing Project and a 1st-year composition instructor at UC Davis, sat down with a group of secondary teachers. Stokes had the data: Students came to the university unprepared for writing about reading and for intellectual tasks such as analyzing, synthesizing, and arguing. The teachers had the curiosity, energy, and drive to do something about the problem. They just needed to get to the bottom of the matter. What do our students need to be ready for college?

Certainly, students need more than literary analysis skills since literary analysis has a limited run in higher education. That was the first discovery when high school and college teachers sat down together to kick off

Transition to College (T2C), a program that began with a 2-week institute on campus. Teachers from around the Sacramento area immersed themselves in all the ins and outs of 1st-year college reading and writing assignments. One of the high school teachers, Jayne Marlink, describes the scene.

> If you had walked into the room, you would not have known what was going on. There were college readers all over the tables. We wanted to start by getting the texts right, so we were diving in, looking for models, for what would engage kids, for edgy, issue-based themes that pull together reading and writing assignments. We talked constantly about our students. What do they think about? What do they know? We knew that even if the texts we selected were hard as hell to read, the kids would give it a shot if they connected to the topic. (All Marlink quotes in this chapter are from a personal communication, March 28, 2013.)

Ultimately, the teachers collaborated on theme-driven units. Along the way, they encountered firsthand the intellectual and discipline-based work they wanted for their students. They also crafted a set of principles—a kind of mutual pledge—for how to proceed in all their dealings:

- Teachers at all grade levels (in this case high school and college) need to collaborate.
- Teachers ought to be developing curriculum, not just implementing it.
- Students need to see themselves in what they are reading and writing, which calls for more diverse texts.
- Students need to read the kinds of things they are writing.

The T2C curriculum started out literally in a single cardboard box. After the first summer institute, the teachers added more to the box, including student writing. Teachers in subsequent summer institutes started from scratch, but would look at the boxes from the previous groups. In other words, the curriculum was dynamic, always being updated and re-created for the students in the present moment. The guiding principle that students should read and write in the same genre made it easier for teachers to move from a literature-only curriculum to one that included more nonfiction. Marlink, now Executive Director of the California Writing Project, observes that developing curriculum is "not about just gathering stuff. It's about gaining a deep enough understanding of intellectual work so you can explain and illustrate it for students."

The bottom line is that the teachers in this project assumed the authority to do something about access for students to higher education. They worked collaboratively across grade levels, listening to and learning from each other.

"The teachers saw themselves as designers of instruction. No one gave them a script," says Stokes. "They saw their job as creating the best possible curriculum for students who would be the first in their families to go to college."

Thoughts About Teacher Collaboration

It goes without saying that T2C teachers established their own collaborative community where they could ask their most basic questions: Why aren't our kids going to college? What can we do about it? In fact, the whole idea of inquiry permeated this venture. As they were developing units of study, teachers took them into the test-

"Teachers learn by doing, reading, and reflecting (just as students do); by collaborating with other teachers; by looking closely at students and their work; and by sharing what they see" (Darling-Hammond & McLaughlin, 1995, p. 598).

ing ground of the classroom. They watched how students reacted and how they performed. Whatever teachers learned they shared with each other, along with the new questions that popped up during their investigations. This process of working together, trying things out, and coming up with new questions spills over into the classroom. According to Sheridan Blau (1993), "teachers who become researchers, writers, authors—persons who are engaged in the construction of knowledge—will devote themselves to figuring out how to turn their own classrooms into such communities for their students" (p. 17).

When it comes to teacher collaboration, T2C had an uncommonly good feature. Basic writing teachers from the local community college, state university, and University of California were active contributors at the beginning—sharing their units as examples, passing on readings, and clarifying college-writing expectations through reading student work with the high school teachers. Stokes explains: "The postsecondary teachers supported the secondary teachers as valued colleagues on the same journey to prepare students for academic writing. Teachers at both levels changed their assumptions of one another, found commonalities, and enjoyed colleagueship when they came together around the shared mission. The high school–college cross-institutional relationship was a radical change from business as usual" (personal communication, June 5, 2014).

Teachers teaching teachers across grade levels is still a radical notion. When James Gray started the National Writing Project in 1973 at UC Berkeley, he envisioned teachers coming together as a community of scholars—a startling idea because teachers had always occupied such tight quarters, closed-off classrooms where they worked day after day, sometimes without seeing or talking to another adult. If and when they emerged for a breath of fresh air, perhaps at a conference or district meeting, chances were that no one asked them what they thought.

The Writing Project broke new ground for teachers. It recognized their classroom experience and expertise and the fact that they were curious folks, eager to learn more. It provided multiple ways for teachers to convene, to talk across grade levels and disciplines, to conduct research, and to construct knowledge. One of NWP's most important principles is "that all members come to the knowledge-making table with something to share, something to learn, and a desire to inquire into problems together" (Stokes, 2010, p. 160).

Shore and Stokes (2006) highlight the idea of "an intellectual lifeline," as an "antidote to sometimes grinding conditions of schools" (p. 108). They believe as we do that teachers are more likely to thrive when they are part of a "lasting, well-supported professional community knit together by abiding interests in learning more about, and teaching, a subject discipline" (p. 107).

Creating an Intellectual Community

Jerry Halpern started teaching English in 1969 in the Pittsburgh (Pennsylvania) Public Schools. He was one of those teachers who everyone in the district "knows," the way people know of each other—by word of mouth and by reputation and by some kind of teacher-generated "who's who." Halpern was the guy who chaired the English department by sharing the chair, so to speak, as his urban high school developed a democratic approach to decisionmaking. He was the guy district literacy director JoAnne Eresh called on to help revise the ELA curriculum, to participate in the Arts Propel Portfolio Project, and to jump into the New Standards movement. The list of Halpern's 33-year involvement in professional partnerships and programs goes on and on—and all the while, he was a classroom teacher. Halpern credits the vision of district administrators like Eresh and the openness of his teaching colleagues for the leadership and learning opportunities that took students and teachers to new heights.

As Halpern saw it, the kind of professionalism he experienced has some defining characteristics: "a fundamental focus on teaching and learning; a high degree of collegiality and collaboration; a willingness to put yourself and your work forward for examination" (unless otherwise cited, all Halpern quotes in this chapter are from a personal communication, April 10, 2013). In the story that follows, Halpern and his colleagues, buoyed and informed by years of teamwork and participation in various reform efforts, put their own spin on a community of scholars—investigating their theories and practices by throwing open their classroom doors.

Case Study: Creating an Intellectual Community

It's 6:30 a.m. Jerry Halpern puts on the coffee in his classroom as his colleagues drift in to chat. Much of the conversation is social, but teachers can't help it: They always end up talking shop.

Halpern retired several years ago. During his tenure as English Department Chair, he constantly looked for ways to get teachers together, including weekly meetings for talking about the business of teaching. With one of his colleagues, John Davis, he developed a reading/writing workshop curriculum, complete with literacy portfolios.

Before long, Halpern and Davis began observing each other and then, joined by colleague Mona Rush, they came up with the idea of teaching each other's classes. Each worked up a set of minilessons or minicourses and began trading classrooms. Afterward they shared what happened—the good and the not-so-good. "The professional dialogue kept us focused. We were talking about curriculum and student writing and how to use our individual strengths to help these kids," remembers Halpern.

Working together gave Halpern and Davis the courage to take risks. They ventured into the "uncharted territory" of literacy portfolios—a vehicle for students to demonstrate "accomplishment, use of process, and development as readers, writers, and speakers" (Davis & Halpern, 1995, pp. 60, 66). Each quarter, they once again traded classes so that the students could present their work to a teacher other than their own. The two teachers listened to students describe their progress and problems with a more objective ear. For the students, having another audience meant being more detailed and precise in their analysis.

"In the end, we would never have accomplished all we did without each other's support," notes Halpern. "I'm not just talking about what happened in terms of our teaching. I'm also talking about the psychological boost—the confidence we gave each other each time we tried something new."

LAST THOUGHTS

Jerry Halpern exemplifies teachers who connect with colleagues at all points in their careers and, in doing so, are energized, well-informed professionals in the classroom and in the field itself. Their energy and their modeling are not lost on their students. Quite the contrary. Students thrive in a world where learning, and particularly writing, occur in a social context. Like their teachers, they find nourishment and joy from talking to each other.

Many years ago, James Britton (1970) observed: "anyone who succeeded in outlawing talk in the classroom would have outlawed life for the adolescent: the web of human relations must be spun in school as well as out" (p. 223). In many ways, Britton laid down the gauntlet. Students need to interact, regardless of college or career preparation. To keep interaction at bay in the place where adolescents spend an entire day is to withhold important resources and information, and no less than the very air they breathe.

"Alone we can do so little; together we can do so much."—Helen Keller (quoted by Herrmann, 1999)

We didn't make collaboration the topic of this chapter by accident. For too long everything has been about testing individual performance and a kind of John Wayne—"every man for himself"—approach to growth and achievement.

Certainly we want students to be able to read and write independently—but not every waking minute and not to the exclusion of working profitably with others. Both research and daily reality point to the virtues and absolute necessity of teamwork. The alternative seems no longer possible in a complex, interconnected world. "Competition without collaboration promotes closed systems. It closes classroom doors and prevents innovation and new ideas" (Bevacqua, 2013).

The big secret behind successful collaboration is that it happens on all fronts: among students, among students and their teachers, and among teachers themselves. Collaboration is not something to be rationed or treated like a one-time dose of medicine for a select group of recipients. It needs to be more than a footnote, both in the classroom with students and in professional development sessions with teachers. All members of the community—students and teachers alike—deserve to be part of the action with mutual opportunities to inquire, contribute, learn, and work together.

CHAPTER 6

Turning Reform Inside Out

When Edna Shoemaker sailed into an urban high school in Sacramento, California, she pledged to get her students ready for college. As one of the "gang of five," a group of teachers who transferred to this high school in the fall of 1990, Shoemaker challenged her students "to write more, write in different ways, and demonstrate their critical thinking" (all Shoemaker quotes in this chapter are from a personal communication, September 3, 2014).

It was an ideal time for knowledgeable, determined teachers to work together, according to Jayne Marlink, who instigated the group's transfer. "On one hand, we were jazzed because of the Transition to College curriculum we had been developing for several years. [See Chapter 5 for a description of the T2C program.] On the other hand, we had just finished scoring student writing on the district proficiency test. The students in our new high school had come up very short" (all Marlink quotes in this chapter are from a personal communication, September 5, 2014).

At first students were leery of the new, tougher, T2C classes. "It took a while," said Shoemaker, "but gradually students sought out the more demanding classes." One moment of truth was when Shoemaker's 12th-graders, having read one Shakespeare play, asked to read a second. "They saw Shakespeare as the currency of college," Shoemaker explains, "and they wanted to be on board."

But there was another, perhaps more subtle, dynamic at play here. It seemed that high expectations and rigorous academic demands actually built confidence so students could step into the next challenge. "They discovered they could do hard things and they could understand things for themselves," Shoemaker explains.

Shoemaker also felt she could do hard things, thanks to the T2C program.

> I was not handed a box of what I was supposed to teach. We developed a curriculum that matched our students and our vision for them. For example, we wanted our students to think critically about literature in general, to consider what it takes for a piece of literature to be a classic. After they read *Their Eyes Are Watching God*, we had

them read a Richard Wright essay that excoriated the book and an Alice Walker essay that found it of great value. Then the students had to argue whether this should still be a core novel at our high school.

"Part of being in the 'gang of five' is that I was given permission to take risks and missteps," says Shoemaker. "We were a community of learners together, teachers and students. The rule was to tell the truth about how we learn, why we learn, and what makes it hard to learn."

In fact, Shoemaker and her colleagues had an abundance of what it takes to move students who were traditionally not enrolled in college prep classes in the direction of college and satisfying careers. They based the curriculum on themes that affected their students' lives. They included a substantial amount of nonfiction and taught a range of writing, "some personal, some text-based, with an emphasis on analysis, synthesis, research, and argument." Their units helped students move from personal to analytical writing, and

> The classroom should be what it is trying to foster. (Eisner, 1985, p. 365)

paid "special attention to the study of the demands and culture of college" (Center for Research and Extension Services for Schools, 2000, p. 61). They also had the benefits of professional collaboration and leaders in their ranks, particularly those like Marlink who knew an opportunity when she saw one and started an influx of great teachers into high schools that needed them most. As Shoemaker said, the ticket to learning is to work together—teachers and students alike—and to be thoughtful about how and why we learn.

TAKING THE PLUNGE:
TEACHERS IN THE LEAD

What stands out for us in this story is that teachers seized on the idea of working from the *inside* to give their students a first-class ticket to their next destination. Shoemaker and her colleagues are, of course, among thousands of teachers who have pulled out all the stops for their students, figuring out how to put college and career in their futures. Their success illustrates once again that teachers are at the center of change. In the thoughtful hands of great teachers, classrooms and whole schools can be transformed.

But this kind of transformation does not happen when teachers are on what Elliot Eisner (1985) calls "the assembly line." According to Eisner, "if one is primarily interested in control and measured outcome, the best way to do it is to disallow the adventitious, to focus attention on highly discrete and highly defined tasks and to assess after each task in order to determine whether the objectives of the tasks have been achieved" (p. 20).

Furthermore, teachers in the classroom today are bound to come up against interpretations of the Common Core that could push them toward one extreme or another. Too often these interpretations defy common sense. For example, the CCSS directs students to "cite specific textual evidence when writing or speaking to support conclusions drawn from the text." In her article "Reading Is About More Than Evidence," Mia Hood (2014) notes how this focus has the potential, if slavishly followed, to drastically alter the way we read: "The trouble is that when students read in this way, they don't recognize all that text does and can do besides serving as evidence. The first standard doesn't acknowledge the way text elicits thinking and draws out new ideas, curiosities, frustrations, causes, and sometimes even pursuits" (para. 12).

While no one can anticipate every possible anomaly that might surface around the Common Core, what seems most important is to encourage teachers to take their rightful place as leaders and professionals. To this end, we will revisit the CCSS for writing with a slightly different lens, first by reminding ourselves again about what the standards mean and don't mean. And then we will make the case that teachers are the main players in this era of reform.

DIVING DEEPER:
SOME REMINDERS OF WHAT'S WHAT

The CCSS are not a curriculum. They provide a flexible kind of road map for teaching writing and identify ultimate destinations, but they do not require a particular route for getting there.

Misinterpretations of the standards pop up routinely, and over and over again, like weeds. The idea that the CCSS are a curriculum is one of them. The CCSS anchor standards do prioritize key concepts and skills that are fundamental to writing and map out some of what learners should be able to accomplish. As destinations, the anchor standards are must-sees. But a curriculum also has content, teaching and learning activities, projects, simulations, reading and video materials, assignments, assessments, planned events, and so on. Don't be fooled or persuaded that standards and curriculum mean the same thing. Just as you would work with your students on the credibility of their sources, keep an eye on the claims and promises that are sure to accompany the next generation of resources and materials.

Without a doubt, production of canned curricula will continue. And even worse, publishers and others will develop a required reading list in the name of Common Core. Buyers beware: There is no CCSS required reading list. In his opinion piece "The Conservative Case for Common Core," William Bennett (2014) notes that "textbook companies have marketed their books disingenuously, leading many parents to believe that under Common Core the government mandates particular textbooks. Also not true" (p. A11).

Another "weed in the garden" is the idea that the grade-level standards for the three types of writing identified in the CCSS are step-by-step recipes for good writing. For instance, the grade 8–level standard for argumentative writing states that students should be able to "acknowledge and distinguish . . . claim(s) from alternate or opposing claims" by grade 8 (CCSSO & NGA, 2010, p. 42). What it *doesn't* say is that all good arguments *require* the acknowledgment of opposing claims. Once again, it's a matter of fending off misinterpretations, particularly those that would standardize teaching and learning and writing itself.

The CCSS focus on college and career ready skills in reading, writing, speaking, and listening serves a particular function in today's climate, spurred on as it is by economic factors and business needs. But school should never be just a preparation for the next grade level or for some unknown job. School is not just about skills, or as Eisner (1985) says, "about being able to swim four laps of the pool to be able to swim in the deep end" (p. 117). School is about the present moment. It's about discovery, surprises, engagement, conversations, learning from peers, following passions, and participating right now in being a citizen.

> Being college and career ready is not the only goal of education.

School is also about the qualities of mind and characteristics of humanity we wish to foster. Consider the habits of mind in Figure 6.1 deemed "essential for success in college writing," and we would say for success in life as well (Council of Writing Program Administrators, the National Council of Teachers of English, and the National Writing Project, 2011, p.1).

Figure 6.1. Habits of Mind Needed for Success in College Writing

- Curiosity: the desire to know more about the world.
- Openness: the willingness to consider new ways of being and thinking in the world.
- Engagement: a sense of investment and involvement in learning.
- Creativity: the ability to use novel approaches for generating, investigating, and representing ideas.
- Persistence: the ability to sustain interest in and attention to short- and long-term projects.
- Responsibility: the ability to take ownership of one's actions and understand the consequences of those actions for oneself and others.
- Flexibility: the ability to adapt to situations, expectations, or demands.
- Metacognition: the ability to reflect on one's own thinking as well as on the individual and cultural processes used to structure knowledge.

(*Note.* List taken from the *Framework for Success in Postsecondary Writing* developed collaboratively by the Council of Writing Program Administrators, the National Council of Teachers of English, and the National Writing Project, 2011, p.1.)

Whether or not certain qualities of mind guarantee that students will write well in college, they are undoubtedly important parts of every student's education. The bottom line is that a curriculum should not get completely skewed toward one thing or another—college and career prep or test readiness or overemphasis on one subject like reading or math to the exclusion of others. Diane Ravitch (2013), now a critic of current public policies, provides this blueprint for a good education:

> All children need the chance to develop their individual talents. And all need the opportunity to learn the skills of working and playing and singing with others. Whatever the careers of the twenty-first century may be, they are likely to require creativity, thoughtfulness, and the capacity for social interaction and personal initiative, not simple routine skills. All children need to be prepared as citizens to participate in a democratic society. (p. 241)

Whereas Ravitch is concerned that schools will shrink the curriculum to training only for job and college, rather than aiming for good thinkers and good citizens, educational philosopher John Dewey's interest was in the nature of school itself. Dewey (1893) challenges the idea that school exists simply to prepare students for some future endeavor: "if I were asked to name the most needed of all reforms in the spirit of education, I should say: "Cease conceiving of education as mere preparation for later life, and make of it the full meaning of the present life" (p. 660).

Probably every one of us, sometime during our school years, wondered why we had to suffer through a particular torture just so we could be ready for the next torture in the next class or grade. School has to be more than getting ready, getting by, or getting through. A 7th-grader once told us that she really liked school—"But it just eats up so much of the day," she said wistfully. And don't we know it! We hardly need to remind teachers of the hours spent in school, nor of the need to make those hours meaningful at the moment.

Recently, a gaggle of 1st-graders passed in front of us on their way out of the fire station, all of them sporting plastic fire hats. They formed a crooked, meandering line as they looked back at the fire trucks. Some of those children may one day become firefighters because of their field trip. For some, the trip will be just a nice, perhaps somewhat blurry memory. But at that moment, when the children patted their heads to check on their hats (and almost all of them did), there was pure joy and, we guess, a good amount of learning.

Teachers are a special population. Almost everyone has had one, if not many, and certainly everyone seems to have an opinion about them. We checked out an array of bumper stickers aimed at teachers and teaching. In some sense, they all seem to be reacting to a public

Teachers are at the heart of the matter.

perception about what teachers do and how they do it. Here are some familiar examples:

Teachers do it better.

If you think education is expensive, try ignorance.

I'm a teacher . . . What's your superpower?

I teach for the outcome, Not the income.

Those who can, Teach. Those who cannot pass laws about teaching.

Warning: Driver may be grading papers.

If you can read this—thank a teacher.

The bumper sticker we like best is this one: "Amazing teacher in action." Who else in the world has to take charge all day long, make decisions, tackle problems, work with students, collaborate with colleagues, design curriculum, create lesson plans, assess progress, showcase student accomplishments, communicate with parents, attend meetings, supervise clubs and activities, participate in committees, rearrange classroom furniture, and by the way, be kind, considerate, sensitive, entertaining, and stimulating? And there's one more thing. Teachers hold the key to deep and lasting changes in education.

The story that follows comes from the field of medicine, but it can be applied to education. Think about "amazing teachers in action" and what it takes to make improvements in teaching and learning: It takes the people on the ground who bring essential knowledge and wisdom to any kind of reform.

THE POWER OF POSITIVE DEVIANCE

In his book *Better: A Surgeon's Notes on Performance,* Atul Gawande (2007) describes an age-old problem with hospital infections in our country and names the culprit: lack of proper hand washing. His story takes place at a veterans hospital in Pittsburgh, Pennsylvania, where those in command made every possible move to encourage hand washing, from educating and scolding to bringing in engineers to install gel dispensers in each hospital room. Still, alarmingly, the infections persisted and, in some cases, medical personnel rebelled against all the outside forces telling them what to do.

It seemed, then, that even the best, most innovative solutions brought into the hospital failed to produce lasting change. But the belief that things could be turned around did not disappear. One of the hospital surgeons had read about *positive deviance*—the idea of working from the inside, building on capabilities people already have instead of bringing in outside "experts" to tell them how they need to change. In March 2005, health care workers on every level—food service workers, janitors, nurses, doctors, and even patients—came together in a series of small-group discussions. The leaders, headed by the surgeon, introduced the session by saying, "We're here because of the hospital infection problem and we want to know what *you* know about how to solve it."

What happened next is a solid testimony to the power of positive deviance:

> Ideas came pouring out. People told of places where hand-gel dispensers were missing, ways to keep gowns and gloves from running out of supply, nurses who always seem able to wash their hands, and even taught patients to wash their hands too. Many people said it was the first time anyone had ever asked them what to do. The norms began to shift. When forty new hand-gel dispensers arrived, staff members took charge of putting them in the right places. Nurses who would never speak up when a doctor failed to wash his or her hands began to do so after learning of other nurses who did. (Gawande, 2007, p. 26)

This "*inside* team" conducted the follow-through, posting monthly results. All the ideas got publicity on the hospital website and in newsletters. "One year into the experiment—and after years without widespread progress—the entire hospital saw its MRSA [antibiotic resistant bacteria, *Methicillin-resistant Staphylococcus aureus*] wound infection rates drop to zero," Gawande explains (pp. 26–27).

So what made the difference? It was positive deviance. It was an unbeatable approach to making change: empowering the people-in-the-know and investing in their knowledge and abilities.

The teachers whose stories we have recounted in this book are shining examples of positive deviance. When Edna Shoemaker joined "the gang of five" in her Sacramento high school, she was fairly new to the profession. "At that time, I was still trying to find my way as a teacher," she says. But she and her four colleagues set their sights on sending students to college and then figured out everything they needed to do to make it happen, using each other as resources and bringing in what they had learned from other colleagues who taught in college.

Remember Jerry Halpern and John Davis, the two Pittsburgh, Pennsylvania teachers who started out observing each other and then decided to teach each other's classes? From these beginnings, Halpern and Davis felt confident to take more risks, to talk frankly about successes and failures, to take on the challenge of literacy portfolios, and ultimately, to involve the entire English department in reflective discussions. They exemplify positive deviance at its best: building their own capacities so they and their colleagues could make steady improvements in their teaching.

Tracy Freyre and her colleagues were positive deviants when they worked together to create a unit for English language learners that built on what they knew about their students, on their combined knowledge of how to scaffold, and on what they found out when they tried out their own assignment. So while they were building their students' abilities, they were also building their own abilities as teachers.

When Stan Pesick invited teachers to ask their own questions about the teaching and learning of argumentative writing, he created a community of positive deviants. From those questions, teachers developed a series of lessons to test out in their own classrooms. This approach puts teachers in charge of working through all the necessary steps, the ins and outs of what it takes to teach *their* students to write arguments. Pesick put it this way: "Rather than inviting in an outside person, teachers drive their own professional development" (personal communication, March 18, 2014).

Judy Kennedy wanted seniors to know what it means to be a good citizen. Instead of lecturing at length from her own experience and expertise, she sent them out in the world to tackle local problems that needed fixing. An act of positive deviance. Liz Harrington wanted her middle schoolers to learn about literary analysis. Instead of locking them into a traditional form of writing, she hooked them on blogging where they learned and practiced the features of analysis. She built on their capacities to communicate with each other through social media. An act of positive deviance. Zack Lewis-Murphy bypassed other less inspiring, skill-based exercises when he plunged his struggling 7th-graders into a writing task that built on their common knowledge about food. An act of positive deviance.

And then there are the two Jims. Jim Gray bucked tradition when he started the Writing Project, placing his faith in teachers and in their capacities to grow and to help each other grow. He tracked down successful writing teachers "who knew and believed in what they were doing," and who could teach their colleagues if given the opportunity:

> I knew that the knowledge successful teachers had gained through their experience and practice in the classroom was not tapped, sought after, shared, or for the most part, even known about. I knew also that if there was ever going to be reform in American education, it was going to take place in the nation's classrooms. And because teachers—and no one else—were in those classrooms, I knew that for reform to succeed, teachers had to be at the center. (Gray, 2000, p. 50)

As for Jim Moffett, he was not walking on a world stage when he dared to define a universe of discourse for a worldwide audience of teachers and university faculty members. As a visionary and pioneer, he challenged the curriculum of the day and threw open the doors for what was possible in the teaching of writing. Regina Foehr (1997) provides more evidence that Jim Moffett was a positive deviant:

In academia, we too often take ourselves too seriously and don't look at the lighter side, sometimes even fear reprisal if we explore the unconventional or write what we really believe. We favor instead the safety of tradition. When Jim and I talked about his willingness to follow his intuition beyond the safety of established boundaries—to write, for example, on unconventional topics—he always modestly downplayed any particular courage. He seemed to think he simply enjoyed a freedom of expression as an independent writer that institutional affiliation would have denied him. (p. 6)

BRINGING POSITIVE DEVIANCE
TO THE COMMON CORE STATE STANDARDS

Unlike Jim Moffett, most of us work within institutions where it sometimes takes special courage to map out a route that makes sense for our students. Being a positive deviant is not always so easy. It seems to us, however, that the CCSS make way for teachers to build their own writing curriculum and to grow their own expertise. And in fact, they provide a solid defense for doing so.

Let's take one more look at the CCSS—through the eyes of a positive deviant. The CCSS have goals we can believe in. We want all students to be ready for and successful in college and careers. The CCSS leave teaching to teachers. That's us, the people on the inside and at the heart of the matter. The CCSS identify uncommonly good ideas for the curriculum teachers will develop, like integrating reading, writing, speaking, and listening, and uncommonly good ideas for teaching writing, like paying attention to purpose and audience. What's more, the good ideas have a long track record in writing classrooms. They are not from outer space. They endure because they work. Teachers discovered them long ago and over the years have helped each other learn to use them effectively.

We have called these good ideas "must-sees" because they are the main attractions, the five-star, not-to-be-missed approaches to teaching writing. They show up in the Common Core unfettered by scripts or pacing guides. Teachers can decide, for example, when and for how long their students need to practice a particular kind of writing or a process like revision. It's the must-sees that distinguish the CCSS.

Are there drawbacks to the CCSS? Sure. Their very existence causes the fur to fly. Anytime bureaucrats formulate a blanket set of standards, rules, or policies, you can count on a backlash, not to mention zealots on one side or another who take every word literally or pull words out of context. But nothing can eliminate the teacher:

Once the important concepts and generalizations are identified at a national level for a particular field of study, the way in which they are transformed into an operational curriculum for students is a task for the teacher or the faculty of the school. In this way both national and local needs can be met." (Eisner, 1985, p. 139)

In case Eisner's theory seems disingenuous given the last decade or more of what stood for reform, take a second look. The writers of the CCSS ELA may not have sent out engraved invitations to teachers, but they surely put their money on giving teachers the authority to teach. The CCSS "let teachers teach" is more than a tip of the hat. It's an authentic, bonafide recognition of who is central to the whole enterprise of education. Every time a group of students reads, talks, and writes about different cultures and values, about human suffering and resilience, about the planet Earth or the solar universe, there is an amazing teacher in action who has planned, taught, and orchestrated the lesson. Every time a group of students tries on a new kind of writing or a new way of thinking, there is a teacher cracking open another door or opportunity for those students to get ahead.

But of course teachers don't have to go it alone. Positive deviance in communities like the Writing Project means providing places for teachers to look to each other for "existing uncommon, successful behaviors and strategies" (Pascale, Sternin, & Sternin, 2010, p. 196). Often an innovative idea comes from someone who "does not know he or she is doing anything unusual. Yet once the unique solution is discovered and understood, it can be adopted by the wider community and transform many lives" (p. 3).

The bit of truth—that people often don't credit their ingenuity and know-how—is true of many teachers. But this is not a time for modesty nor for holding back what could be an important contribution. If ever there were a time for teachers to work together, it's now.

We urge our colleagues to take the plunge and dive a little deeper during this era when writing has made a comeback. Be fearless. Explore those must-sees. This is the moment to build your own and your students' capacities in the positive deviant way. And remember to share what you learn. Keep those professional conversations going. We can never have too many.

References

Ackerman, D. (1989, November 12). O muse! You do make things difficult! *New York Times on the Web*. Retrieved from www.nytimes.com/books/97/03/02/reviews/ackerman-poets.html

American College Testing (ACT). (2007). *Writing Framework for the 2011 National Assessment of Educational Progress*. Washington, DC: National Assessment Governing Board.

Applebee, A. (2002). Alternative models of writing development. In R. Indrisano & J. Squire (Eds.), *Perspectives on writing: Research, theory, and practice* (pp. 90–110). Newark, DE: International Reading Association.

Applebee, A. (2013). Common Core State Standards: The promise and the peril in a national palimpsest. *English Journal, 103*(1), 25–33.

Applebee, A., Langer, J., Wilcox, K., Nachowitz, M., Mastroianni, M., & Dawson, C. (2013). *Writing instruction that works: Proven methods for middle and high school classrooms*. New York, NY: Teachers College Press.

Atwell, N. (1987). *In the middle: Writing, reading and learning with adolescents*. Portsmouth, NH: Boynton/Cook.

Bangert-Drowns, R. L., Hurley, M. M., & Wilkinson, B. (2004). The effects of school-based writing-to-learn interventions on academic achievement: A meta-analysis. *Review of Educational Research, 74*, 29–58.

Bennett, W. (2014, September 11). The conservative case for Common Core. *Wall Street Journal*, p. A11.

Bevacqua, J. (2013, April 12). Collaboration AND competition [Blog post]. Retrieved from connectedprincipals.com/archives/8186

Blau, S. (1993). Constructing knowledge in a professional community. *The Quarterly of the National Writing Project and the Center for the Study of Writing, 15*(1), 16–17, 19.

Blau, S. (2010). Academic writing as participation: Writing your way in. In P. Sullivan, H. Tinberg, & S. Blau (Eds.), *What is "college-level" writing? Vol. 2. Assignments, readings, and student writing samples* (pp. 29–56). Urbana, IL: National Council of Teachers of English.

Britton, J. (1970). *Language and learning*. London, United Kingdom: Allen Lane/Penguin Press.

Bruner, J. (1960). *The process of education*. Cambridge, MA: Harvard University Press.

California Department of Education. (1993). *Writing assessment handbook: High school*, Sacramento, CA: Author.

Caplan, R. (1984). *Writers in training: A guide to developing a composition program for language arts teachers*. Lebanon, IN: Dale Seymour.

Caplan, R. (n. d.). *Showing and not telling: A course within a course.* Unpublished manuscript.

Center for Research and Extension Services for Schools (CRESS). (2000). *CRESS Report.* Davis, CA: School of Education, University of California, Davis.

Chall, J. S., Bissex, G. L., Conard, S. S, & Harris-Sharples, S. (1999). *Qualitative assessment of text difficulty: A practical guide for teachers and writers.* Cambridge, MA: Bookline Books.

Coffey, G. (2012). Literacy and technology: Integrating technology with small group, peer-led discussions of literature. *International Electronic Journal of Elementary Education, 4*(2), 395–405.

College Board. (2006). *Twenty outstanding SAT essays.* New York, NY: Author.

Collier, L. (2011, November). The need for teacher communities: An interview with Linda Darling-Hammond. *The Council Chronicle, 21*(2), 12–14.

Colvin-Murphy, C. (1986). *Enhancing critical comprehension of literary texts through writing.* Paper presented at the National Reading Conference, Austin, TX.

Constitutional Rights Foundation. (n.d.). *The Civic Action Project & Common Core State Standards.* Retrieved April 7, 2014, from www.crfcap.org/images/pdf/cap_ccss_ela.pdf

Cope, B., & Kalantzis, M. (Eds.). (1993). *The powers of literacy: A genre approach to teaching writing.* Pittsburgh, PA: University of Pittsburgh Press.

Council of Chief State School Officers (CCSSO) & the National Governors Association (NGA). (2010). *Common core state standards for English language arts and literacy in history/social studies, science, and technical subjects.* Washington, DC: National Governors Association. Available at *Common Core State Standards Initiative* website at www.corestandards.org/the-standards

Council of Writing Program Administrators, National Council of Teachers of English, & National Writing Project. (2011). *Framework for success in postsecondary writing.* Available at *Council of Writing Program Administrators* website at wpacouncil.org/framework

Darling-Hammond, L. (1996). The quiet revolution: Rethinking teacher development. *Educational Leadership, 53*(6), 4–10. Retrieved from www.ascd.org/publications/educational-leadership/mar96/vol53/num06/The-Quiet-Revolution@-Rethinking-Teacher-Development.aspx

Darling-Hammond, L., & McLaughlin, M. W. (1995, April). Policies that support professional development in an era of reform. *Phi Delta Kappan, 76*(8), 597–604.

Darman, J. (2009). Robert Caro's last LBJ volume. Retrieved from www.newsweek.com/robert-caros-last-lbj-volume-82573

Davis, J. W., & Halpern, J. T. (1995). The portfolio classroom. *Iowa English Bulletin, 43,* 60–66.

Dewey, J. (1893). Self-realization as the moral ideal. *The Philosophical Review, 2*(6), 652–664.

Dewey, J. (1938). *Experience and education.* New York, NY: Macmillan/Collier.

Donovan, M. (2015). Writing tips: Show, don't tell. Retrieved from http://www.writingforward.com/writing-tips/writing-tips-show-dont-tell

Duke, N. K., Pearson, P. D., Strachan, S. L., & Billman, A. K. (2011). Essential elements of fostering and teaching reading comprehension. In S. J. Samuels & A. Farstrup (Eds.), *What research has to say about reading instruction* (4th ed., pp. 51–93). Newark, DE: International Reading Association.

Eisner, E. (1985). *The educational imagination: On the design and evaluation of school programs* (2nd ed.). New York, NY: Macmillan.

Fitzgerald, J., & Shanahan, T. (2000). Reading and writing relations and their development. *Educational Psychologist, 35*(1), 39–50.

Foehr, R. (Ed.). (1997). A tribute to James Moffett. *Journal of the Assembly for Expanded Perspectives on Learning, 3,* 1–12. Retrieved from trace.tennessee.edu/cgi/viewcontent.cgi?article=1044&context=jaepl

Friedman, T. (2013, January 12). Collaborate vs. collaborate. *New York Times.* Retrieved from www.nytimes.com/2013/01/13/opinion/sunday/friedman-collaborate-vs-collaborate.html?_r=1&

Gallagher, K. (2009). *Readicide: How schools are killing reading and what you can do about it.* Portland, MN: Stenhouse.

Gallagher, K. (2011). *Write like this: Teaching real-world writing through modeling and mentor texts.* Portland, MN: Stenhouse.

Gawande, A. (2007). *Better: A surgeon's notes on performance.* New York, NY: Picador.

Gladwell, M. (2008). *Outliers: The story of success.* New York, NY: Back Bay Books/ Little, Brown.

Goldberg, N. (2010). *Writing down the bones: Freeing the writer within.* Boston, MA: Shambhala.

Graham, S., & Harris, K. (2013). Designing an effective writing program. In S. Graham, C. A. MacArthur, & J. Fitzgerald (Eds.), *Best practices in writing instruction,* (2nd ed., pp. 3–25). New York, NY: Guilford Press.

Graham, S., & Perin, D. (2007). *Writing next: Effective strategies to improve writing of adolescents in middle and high school.* New York, NY: Carnegie Corporation.

Gray, J. (2000). *Teachers at the center: A memoir of the early years of the National Writing Project.* Berkeley, CA: National Writing Project.

Herrmann, A. (1991). Anxious, b-l-o-c-k-e-d, and computer phobic: A writing teacher's memoirs. In M. Schwartz (Ed.), *Writer's craft, teacher's art: Teaching what we know* (pp. 179–185). Portsmouth, NH: Boynton/Cook.

Herrmann, D. (1999). *Helen Keller: A life.* Chicago, IL: University of Chicago Press.

Hiebert, E. H., & Kamil, M. L. (2009). *Teaching and learning vocabulary: Bringing research to practice.* Abington, Oxford, United Kingdom: Taylor & Francis e-Library.

Hillocks, G., Jr. (1986). *Research on written composition: New directions for teaching.* Urbana, IL: National Conference on Research in English/ERIC Clearinghouse on Reading and Communications Skills.

Hillocks, G., Jr. (2005). The focus on form vs. content in teaching writing. *Research in the Teaching of English, 40,* 238–248.

Hillocks, G., Jr. (2011). *Teaching argument writing, grades 6–12: Supporting claims with relevant evidence and clear reasoning.* Portsmouth, NH: Heinemann.

Hood, M. (2014). Reading is about more than "evidence." *Education Week, 35*(6). Retrieved from www.edweek.org/ew/articles/2014/10/01/06hood.h34.html

Johnson, C., & Stevens, M. (2002). *Script partners: What makes film and TV writing teams work.* Studio City, CA: Michael Wiese Productions.

Juska, J. (1989). The wall. *The Quarterly of the National Writing Project and the Center for the Study of Writing, 11*(2), 13–19.

Lamott, A. (1995). *Bird by bird: Some instructions on writing and life.* New York, NY: Anchor Books.

Lane, B. (1993). *After "the end": Teaching and learning creative revision.* Portsmouth, NH: Heinemann.

Lane, B. (2007, June 19). *Explode the moment and spark imagination in writing* [Video file]. Retrieved from www.youtube.com/watch?v=KykziiHpyuo

Lane, B. (2011, February 8). *Explode a moment with Barry Lane* [Video file]. Retrieved from www.youtube.com/watch?v=mA9YeKBRaL8

Langer, J. (1984). The effects of available information on responses to school writing tasks. *Research in the Teaching of English, 18*(1), 27–44.

McLeod, S. (2012). Zone of proximal development. *SimplyPsychology.* Retrieved from www.simplypsychology.org/Zone-of-Proximal-Development.html

Merrow, J. (Reporter). (2013, August 13). In defining what public school students should know, teachers wonder "How?" [Audio podcast and transcript]. On *PBS Newshour.* Retrieved from www.pbs.org/newshour/bb/education-july-dec13-commoncore_08-13/

Moffett, J. (1965). I, you, and it. *College Composition and Communication, 16*(5), 243–248.

Moffett, J. (1981). *Active voice: A writing program across the curriculum.* Montclair, NJ: Boynton/Cook.

Moffett, J. (1989a). *Bridges: From personal writing to the formal essay.* (National Writing Project and the Center for the Study of Writing Occasional Paper No. 9). Retrieved from www.nwp.org/cs/public/download/nwp_file/62/OP09.pdf?x-r=pcfile_d

Moffett, J. (1989b). Introduction. In A. H. Dyson (Ed.), *Collaboration through writing and reading* (pp. 21–24). Urbana, IL: National Council of Teachers of English.

Moffett, J., & Wagner, B. J. (1976). *Student-centered language arts and reading, K–13* (2nd ed.). Boston, MA: Houghton Mifflin.

Murray, D. (1985). *A writer teaches writing* (2nd ed.). Boston, MA: Houghton Mifflin.

Myers, M. (1982). *The quality of CWP teaching practices for students at different achievement levels.* Berkeley, CA: Bay Area Writing Project (BAWP), California Writing Project (CWP), Commission for Post Secondary Education (CPEC).

National Commission on Writing. (2003). *The neglected "R": The need for a writing revolution.* New York, NY: College Board.

National Writing Project (with DeVoss, D., Eidman-Aadahl, E., & Hicks, T.). (2010). *Because digital writing matters: Improving student writing in online and multimedia environments.* San Francisco, CA: Jossey-Bass.

National Writing Project, & Nagin, C. (2003). *Because writing matters.* San Francisco, CA: Jossey-Bass.

Nguyen, B. M. (2007). *Stealing Buddha's dinner.* London, UK: Penguin Books.

O'Hagan, M. (2011). Kids battle the lure of junk food. Seattle Times. Retrieved from www.seattletimes.com/pacific-nw-magazine/kids-battle-the-lure-of-junk-food/

Pascale, R., Sternin, J., & Sternin, M. (2010). *The power of positive deviance: How unlikely innovators solve the world's toughest problems.* Cambridge, MA: Harvard Business Press.

Pesick, S. (2005). "Lesson study" and the teaching of American history: Connecting professional development and classroom practice. *Social Studies Review, 44*(2), 43–60.

Peterson, A. (1996). *The writer's workout book: 113 stretches toward better prose.* Berkeley, CA: National Writing Project.

Pollan, M. (2008). *In defense of food.* New York, NY: Penguin Books.

Pollan, M. (2010). Food fight. *Utne Reader.* Retrieved from www.utne.com/Environment /Food-Movement-Michael-Pollan-American-Diet.aspx#axzz2TNm5cT00

Ravitch, D. (2011). *The death and life of the great American school system: How testing and choice are undermining education.* New York, NY: Basic Books.

Ravitch, D. (2013). *Reign of error: The hoax of the privatization movement and the danger to America's public schools.* New York, NY: Alfred A. Knopf.

Reichl, R. (2010). *For you mom, finally.* New York, NY: Penguin Books.

Rogak, L. (2009). Haunted heart: The life and times of Stephen King. Retrieved from www.dailyroutines.typepad.com/daily_routines/writers/

Sahakian, P. (2001). The birth and death of portfolio assessment 1992–2000. In M. A. Smith & J. Juska (Eds.). *The whole story: Teachers talk about portfolios* (pp. 51–58). Berkeley, CA: National Writing Project.

Schoenbach, R., Greenleaf, C., Cziko, C., & Hurwitz, L. (1999). *Reading for understanding: A guide to improving reading in middle and high school classrooms.* San Francisco, CA: Jossey-Bass.

Shanahan, T. (2006). Relations among oral language, reading, and writing development. In C.A. MacArthur, S. Graham, & J. Fitzgerald (Eds.), *Handbook of writing research* (pp. 171–183). New York, NY: Guilford Press.

Shanahan, T. (2013). The common core ate my baby and other urban legends. *Educational Leadership, 70*(4), 10–16.

Shore, L., & Stokes, L. (2006). The Exploratorium leadership program in science education: Inquiry into discipline-specific teacher induction. In B. Achinstein & S. Athanases (Eds.), *Mentors in the making: Developing new leaders for new teachers.* New York, NY: Teachers College Press.

Shulman, L. S. (2004). *The wisdom of practice: Essays on teaching, learning, and learning to teach.* San Francisco, CA: Jossey-Bass.

Skjelbred, R. (2005). Poem: The five-paragraph essay. *The Quarterly of the National Writing Project and the Center for the Study of Writing, 27*(1). Retrieved from www.nwp.org/cs/public/print/resource/2189

Smith, M. (2005). Are you ready for college writing? *The Voice, 10*(3), 1–2. Retrieved from www.nwp.org/cs/public/print/resource/2254

Stigler, J., & Hiebert, J. (1999). *The teaching gap: Best ideas from the world's teachers for improving education in the classroom.* New York, NY: Free Press.

Stokes, L. (1990). How the five-paragraph essay formula inhibits students' development in writing and thinking. *Working Knowledge—Letters on Teaching.* Davis, CA: University of California, Davis, Center for Cooperative Research and Extension Services for Schools.

Stokes, L. (2010). The National Writing Project: Anatomy of an improvement infrastructure. In C. Coburn & M. K. Stein (Eds.), *Research and practice in education: Building alliances, bridging the divide,* pp. 147–162. New York, NY: Rowman & Littlefield.

Swales, J. (1990). *English in academic and research settings.* Cambridge, United Kingdom: Cambridge University Press.

Tierney, R., Caplan, R., Ehri, L., Healy, M. K., & Hurdlow, M. K. (1989). Writing and reading working together. In A. H. Dyson (Ed.), *Collaboration through writing and reading* (pp. 169–209). Urbana, IL: National Council of Teachers of English.

Tierney, R., & Shanahan, T. (1996). Research on the reading–writing relationship: Interactions, transactions, and outcomes. In R. Barr, M. L. Kamil, P. B. Mosenthal, & P. D. Pearson (Vol. Eds.), *Handbook of Reading Research* (Vol. 2, 246–280). Mahwah, NJ: Erlbaum.

Treuhaft, S., & Karpyn, A. (2010). *The grocery gap: Who has access to healthy food and why it matters.* Oakland CA: PolicyLink; Philadelphia, PA: The Food Trust. Retrieved from thefoodtrust.org/uploads/media_items/grocerygap.original.pdf

Truong, M. (2010). Lost in translation [Blog post]. *Saveur,* Retrieved from www.saveur.com/article/Kitchen/Lost-in-Translation

Van Edwards, V. (2012, December 12). Can working in teams build your intelligence? *Forbes.* Retrieved from www.forbes.com/sites/theyec/2012/12/12/can-working-in-teams-build-your-intelligence/

Vygotsky, L. S. (1978). *Mind in society: The development of higher psychological processes.* Cambridge, MA: Harvard University Press.

Whithaus, C. (2005). *Teaching and evaluating writing in the age of computers and high-stakes testing.* Mahwah, NJ: Lawrence Erlbaum Associates.

Williams, S. (2009). *The impact of collaborative, scaffolded learning in K–12 schools: A meta-analysis.* San Jose, CA: Cisco Systems. Retrieved from www.cisco.com/web/about/citizenship/socio-economic/docs/Metiri_Classroom_Collaboration_Research.pdf

Witte, S. (1988). *Some contexts for understanding written literacy.* Unpublished manuscript.

Index

The authors express gratitude for permission to use the following:

Chapter 2, excerpt from "Lost in Translation," [Blog post] by Monique Truong, 2010, Saveur, retrieved from www.saveur.com/article/Kitchen/Lost-in-Translation. Used with permission.

Chapter 2, excerpt from *For You Mom, Finally,* © 2009, 2010, by Ruth Reichl, Penguin Books, New York. Used with permission.

Chapter 2, excerpt from "My First Attempt at Cooking," by Zack Lewis-Murphy, unpublished manuscript, n.d. Used with permission.

Chapter 3, excerpts from *In Defense of Food: An Eater's Manifesto,* by Michael Pollan, 2008, Penguin Books. Used with permission.

Chapter 3, excerpt from "Kids Battle the Lure of Junk Food," by Maureen O'Hagan, *Seattle Times,* 2011, retrieved from http://www.seattletimes.com/pacific-nw-magazine/kids-battle-the-lure-of-junk-food/. Copyright 2011, Seattle Times Company. Used with permission.

Chapter 3, "The Five-paragraph Essay," by Ray Skejelbred, 2005, *The Quarterly of the National Writing Project and the Center for the Study of Writing,* retrieved from www.nwp.org/cs/public/print/resource/2189. Used with permission.

Chapter 4, excerpt from *Writers in Training: A Guide to Developing a Composition Program for Language Arts Teachers,* by Rebekah Caplan, 1984, Lebanon, IN, Dale Seymour. Used with permission.

Chapter 4, Figure 4.1, Writing Scrimmages for Argument, by Rebekah Caplan, unpublished manuscript, n.d. Used with permission.

Chapter 5, Figure 5.1, definitions of civic actions were adapted from materials on the Constitutional Rights Foundation website, http://www.crfcap.org/. Used with permission from Keri Doggett and the Constitutional Rights Foundation.